JSB 592

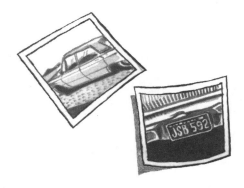

Dear Julia,

Brian BIGGS

TOP SHELF PRODUCTIONS

Dear Julia,

This story was originally published as a four-part series
by Black Eye Books, Montréal, Canada.

Top Shelf Productions
Post Office Box 1282
Marietta, Georgia 30061-1282
WWW . TOPSHELFCOMIX . COM

Written, illustrated and designed by Brian Biggs
WWW . MRBIGGS . COM

First Edition: February 2000
ISBN: 1-891830-12-0

Printed in Canada

one

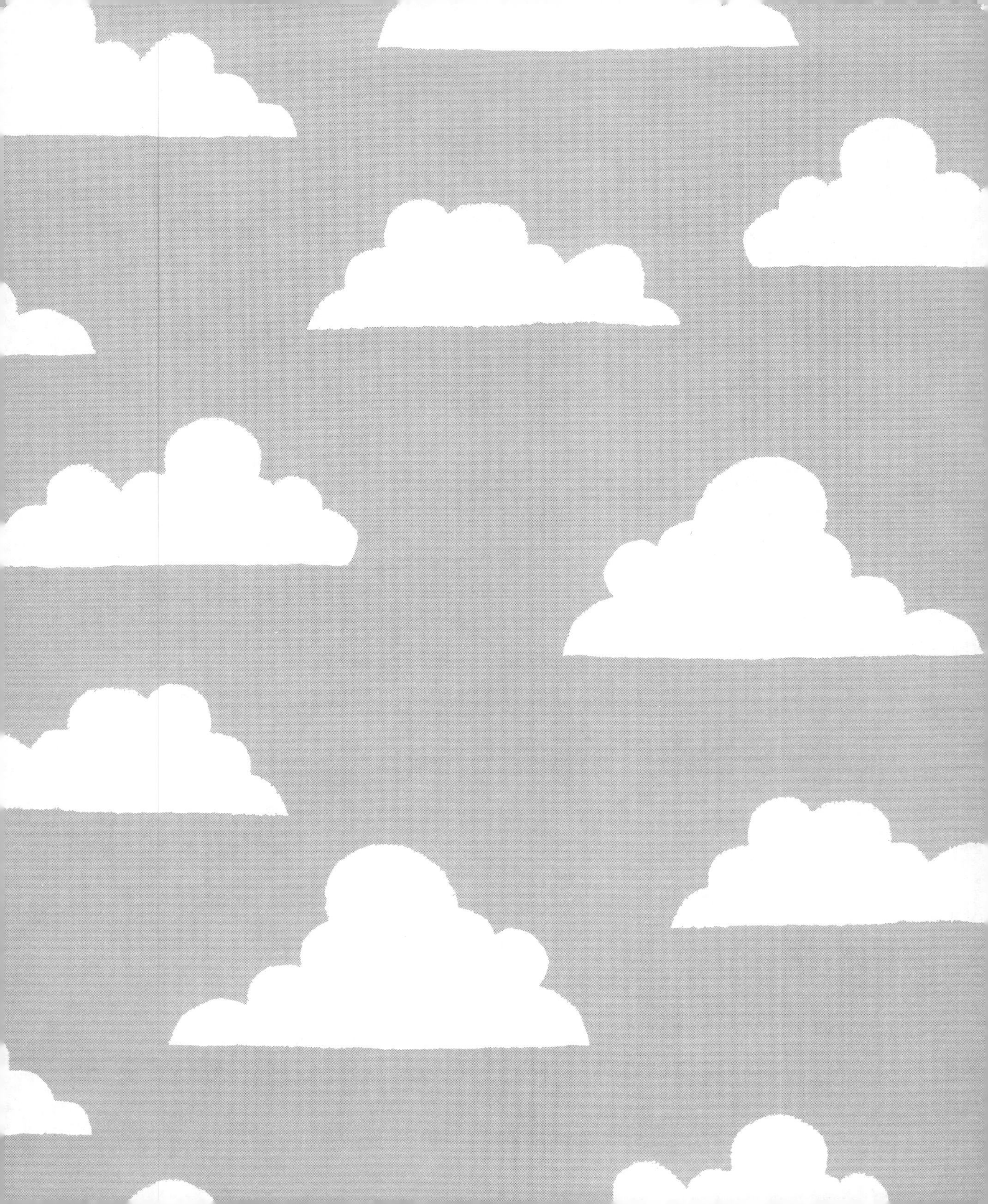

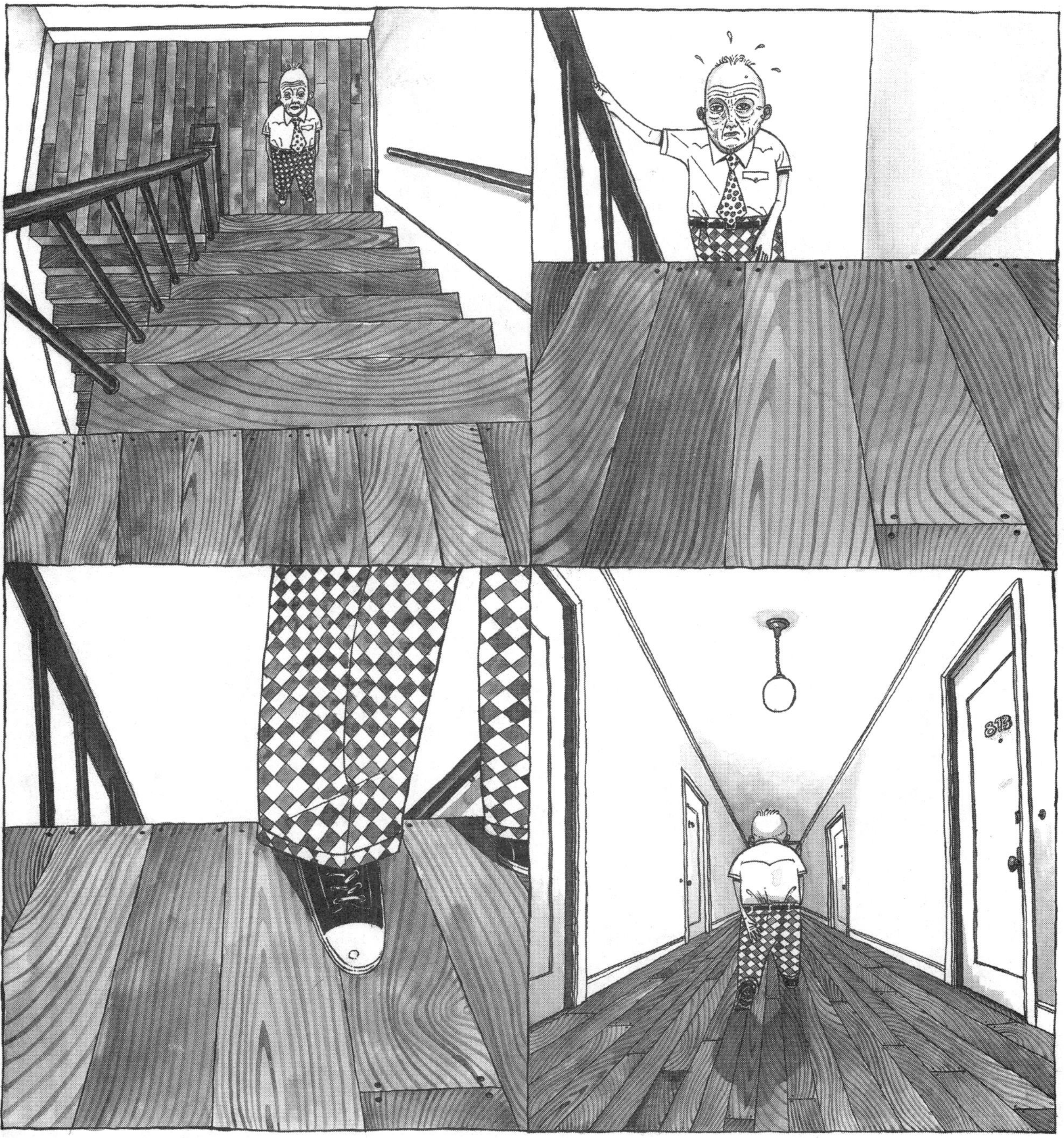
81B

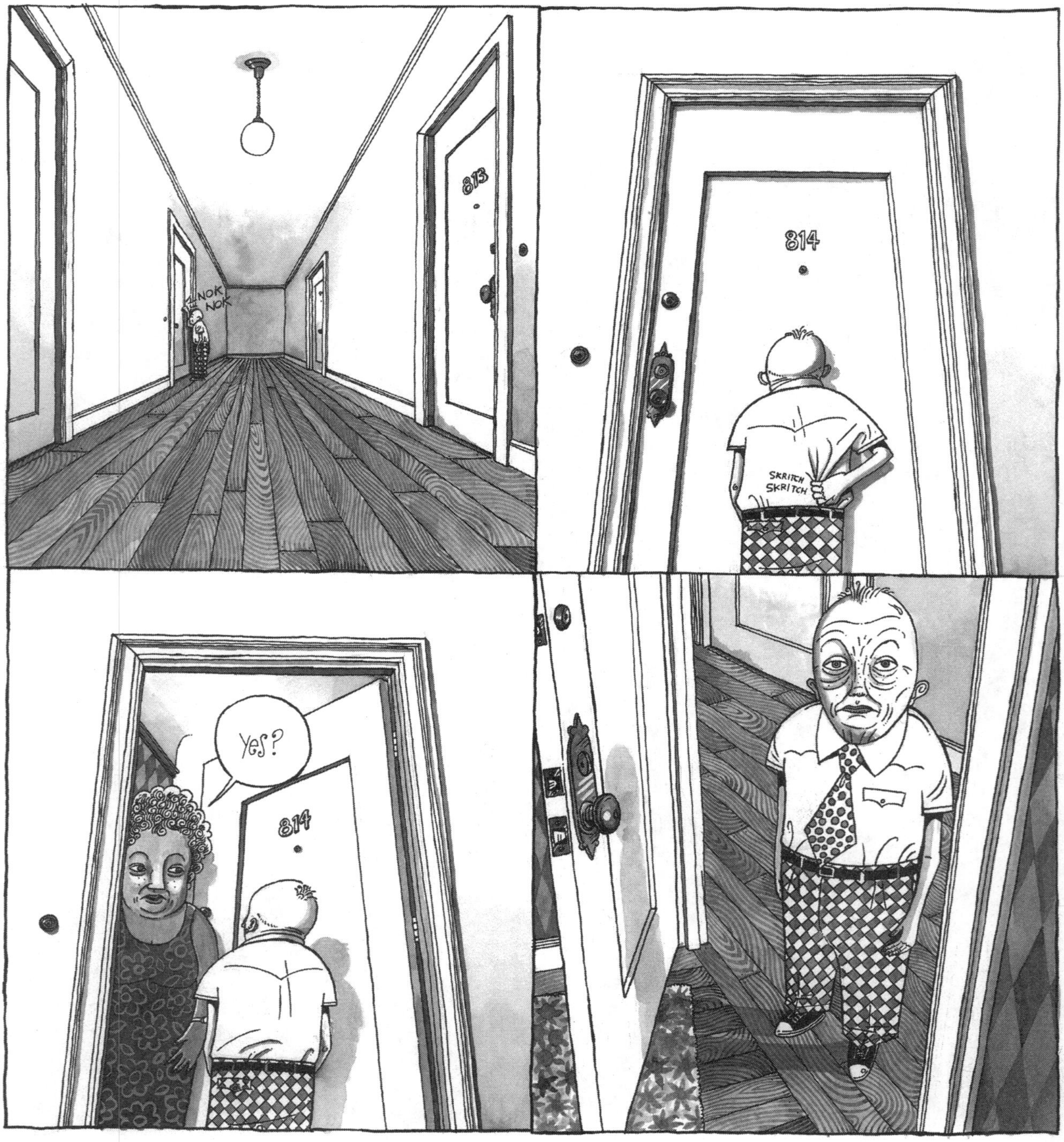

NOK NOK
813
814
SKRITCH SKRITCH
Yes?
814

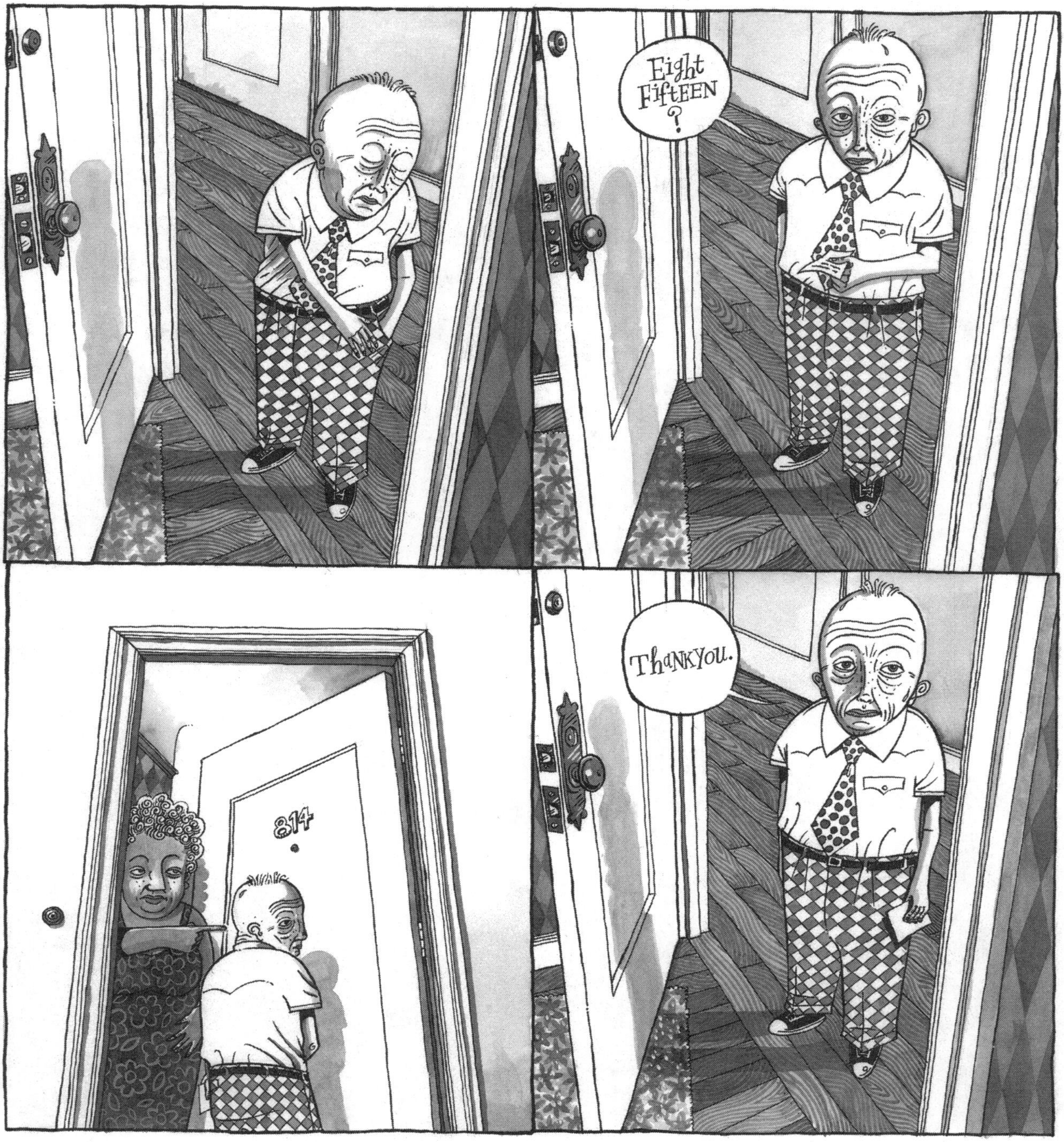

Eight FiftEEN ?
814
ThaNKYOU.

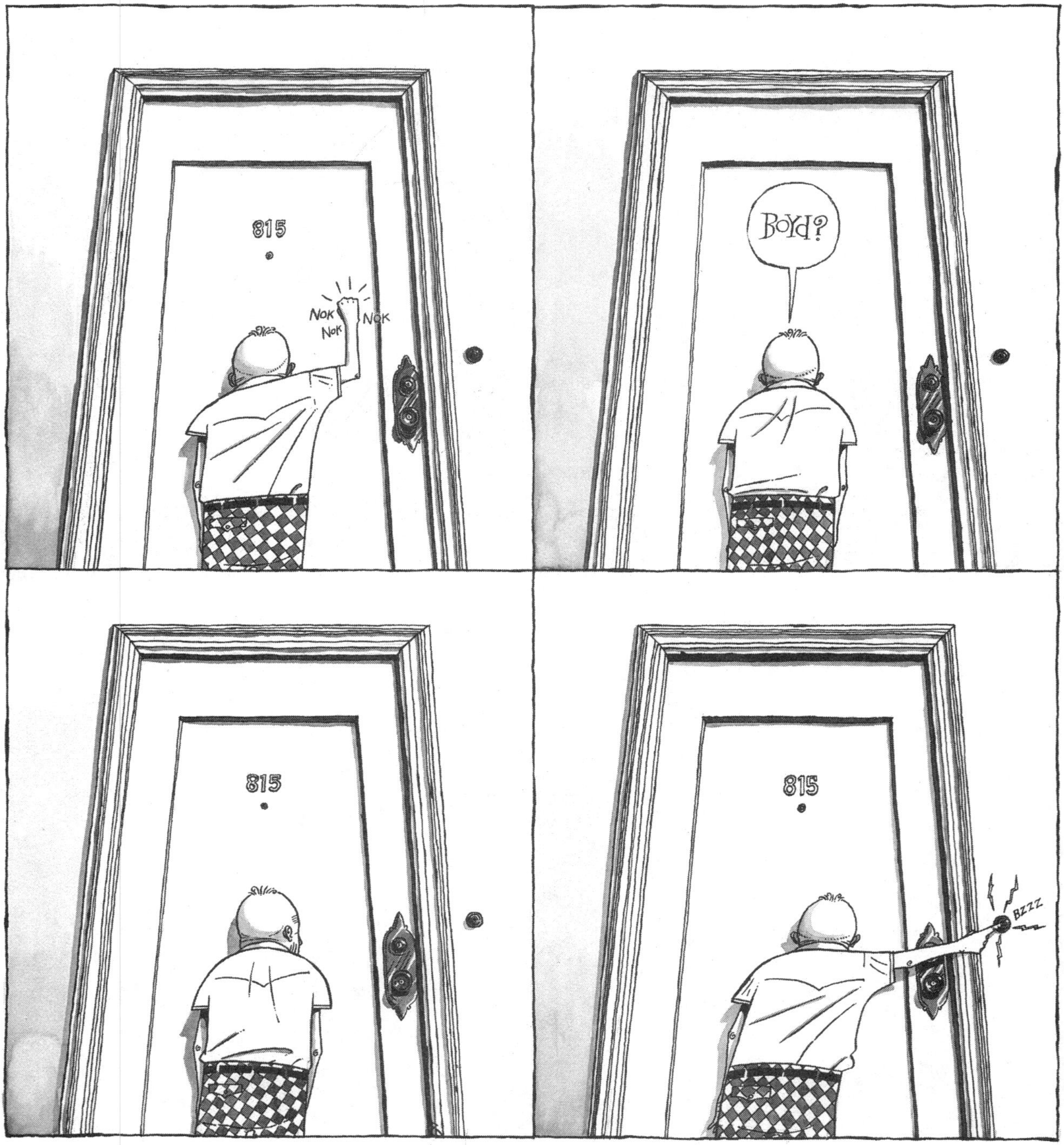
815
NOK
NOK
NOK
BOYD?
815
815
BZZZ

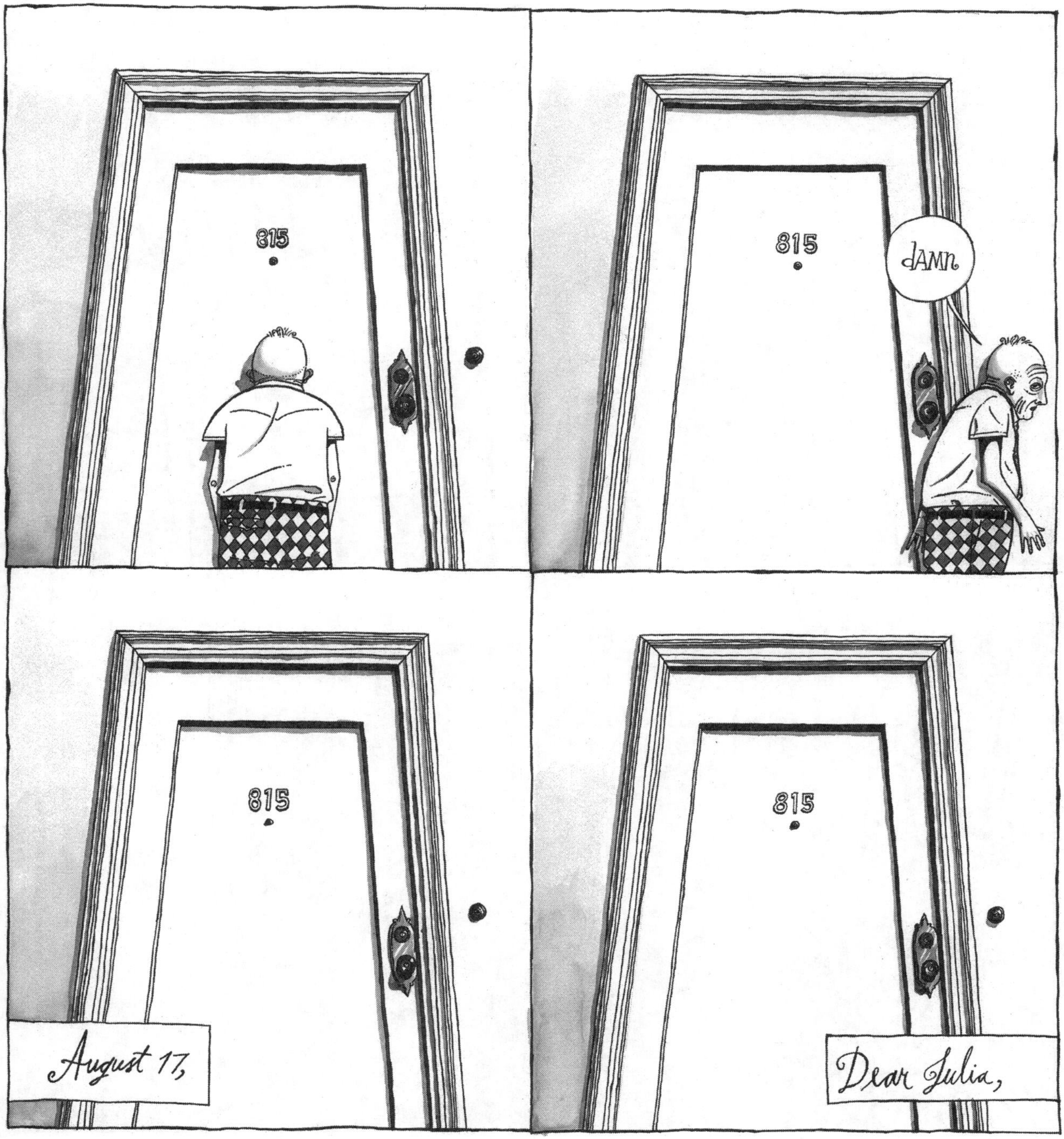
815
815
dAMn
815
August 17,
815
Dear Julia,

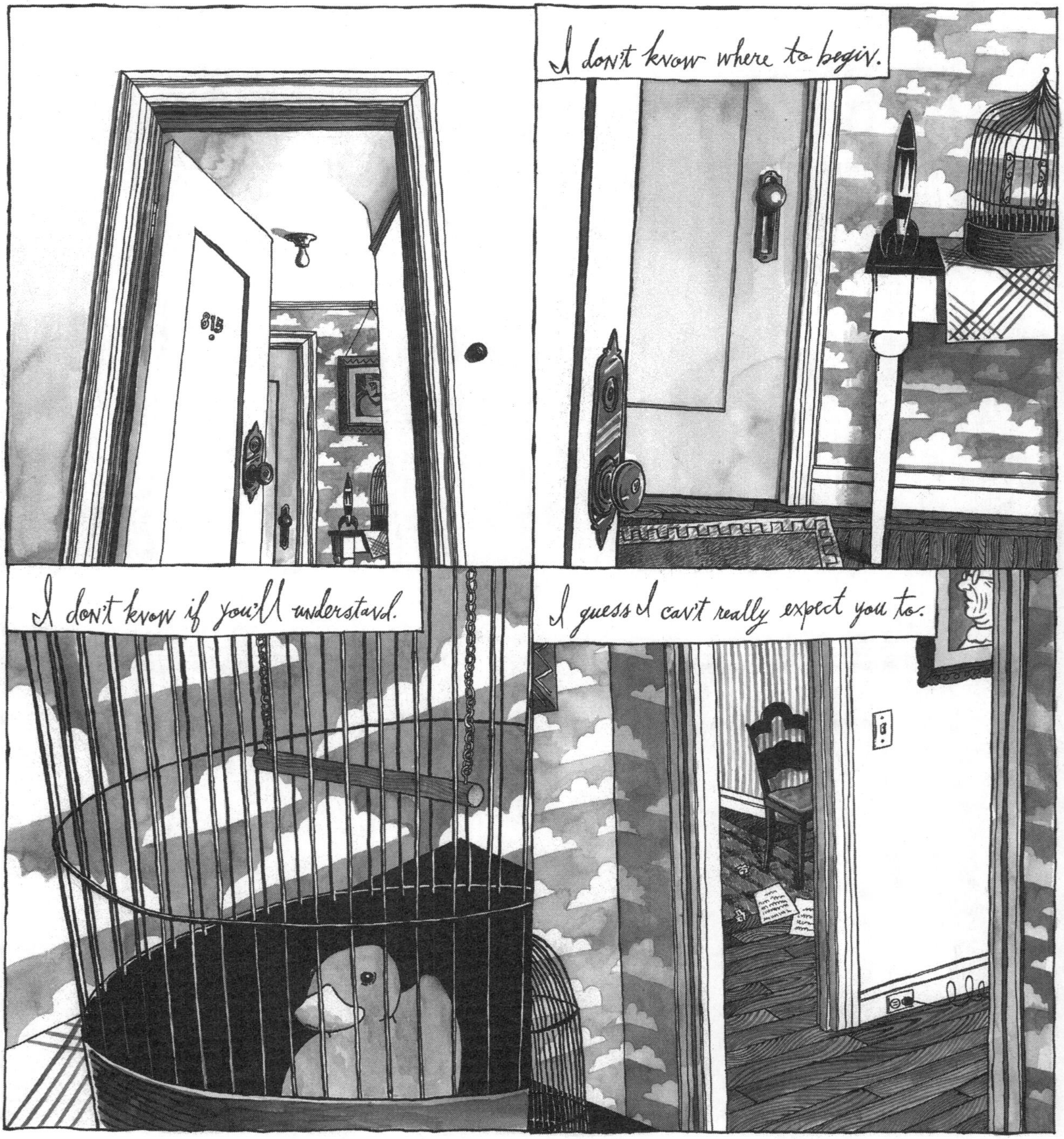
I don't know where to begin.
I don't know if you'll understand.
I guess I can't really expect you to.

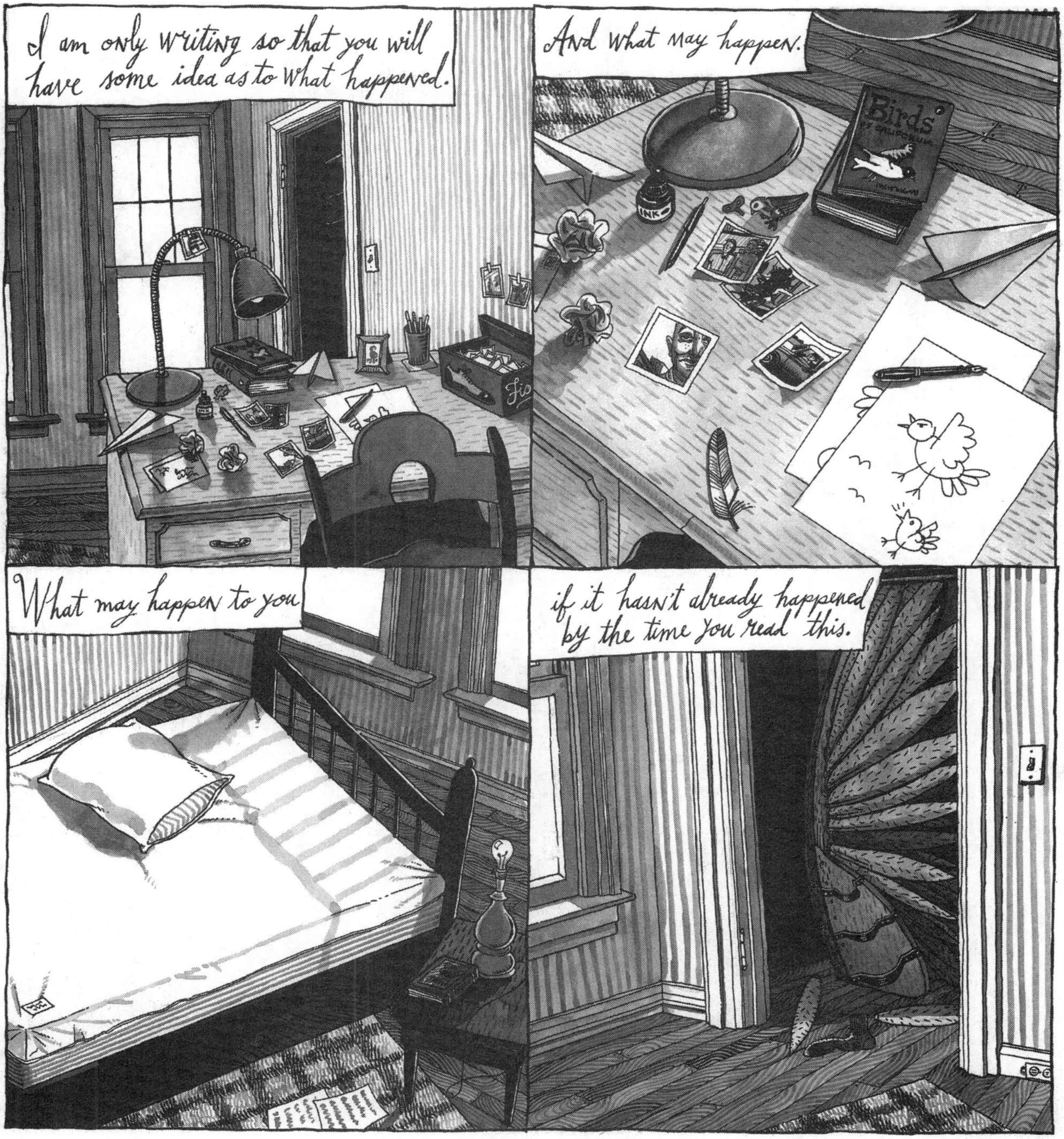
I am only writing so that you will have some idea as to what happened.
And what may happen.
Birds
What may happen to you
if it hasn't already happened by the time you read this.

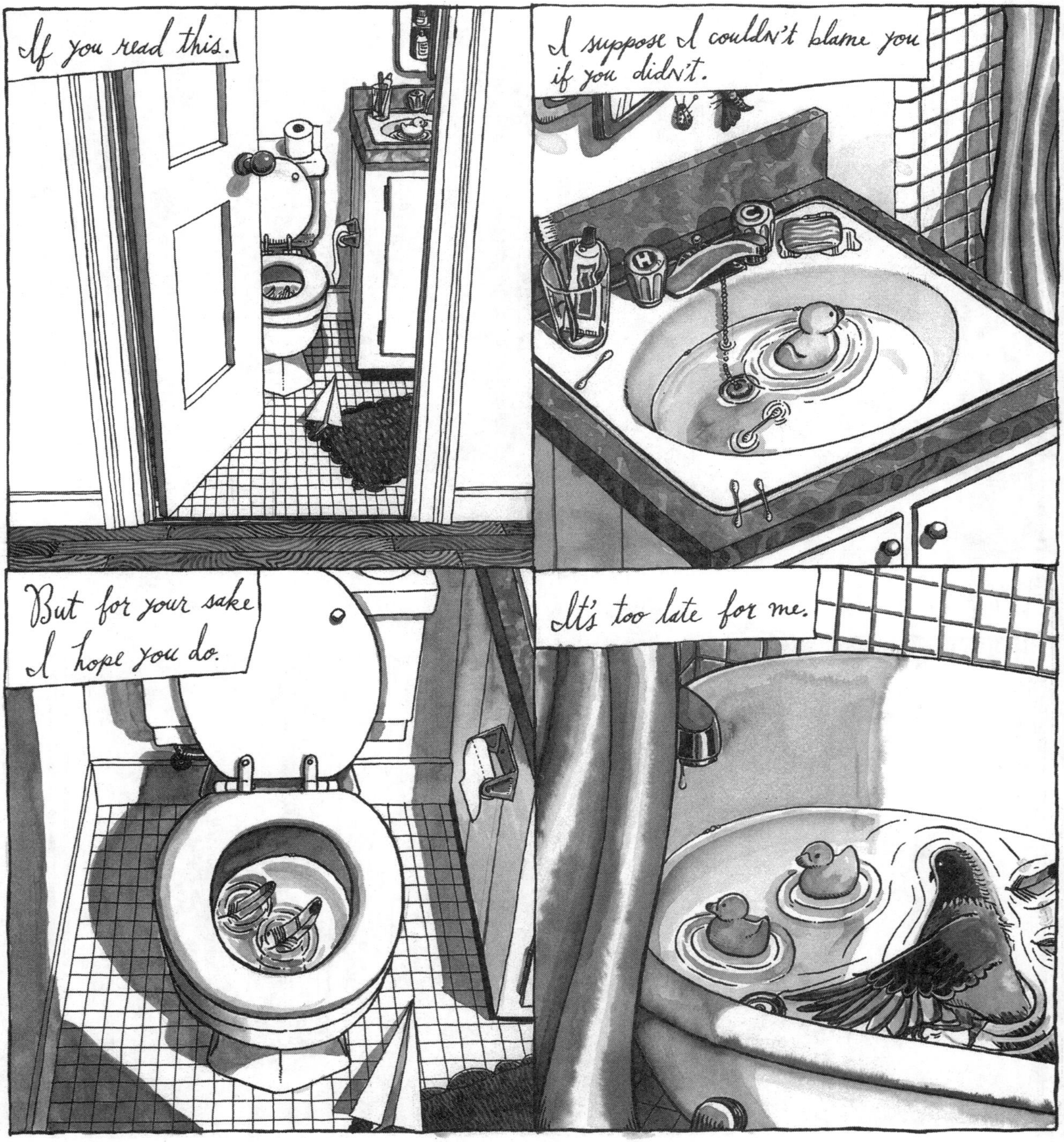
If you read this.
I suppose I couldn't blame you if you didn't.
But for your sake I hope you do.
It's too late for me.

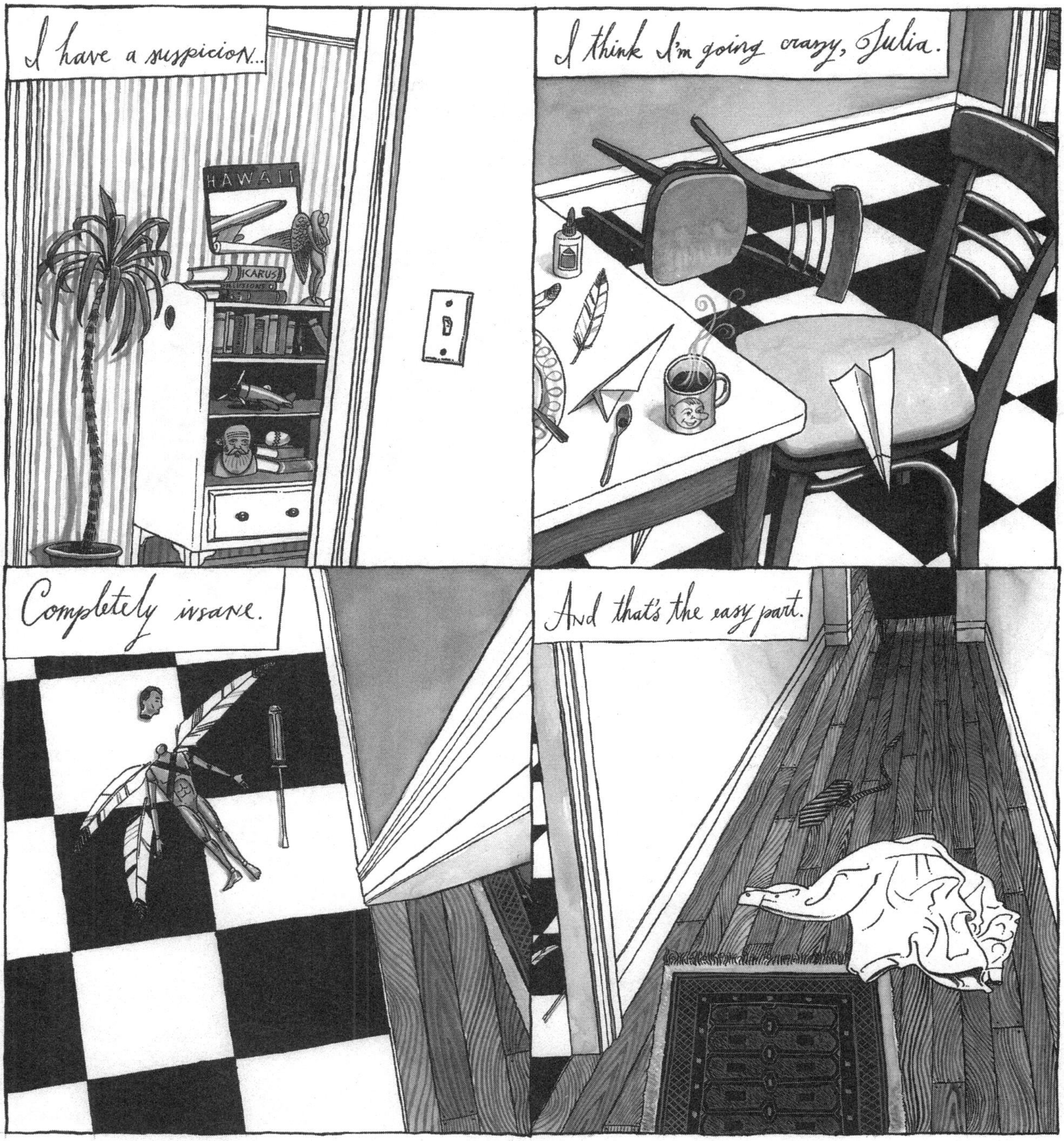
I have a suspicion...
HAWAII
ICARUS
I think I'm going crazy, Julia.
Completely insane.
And that's the easy part.

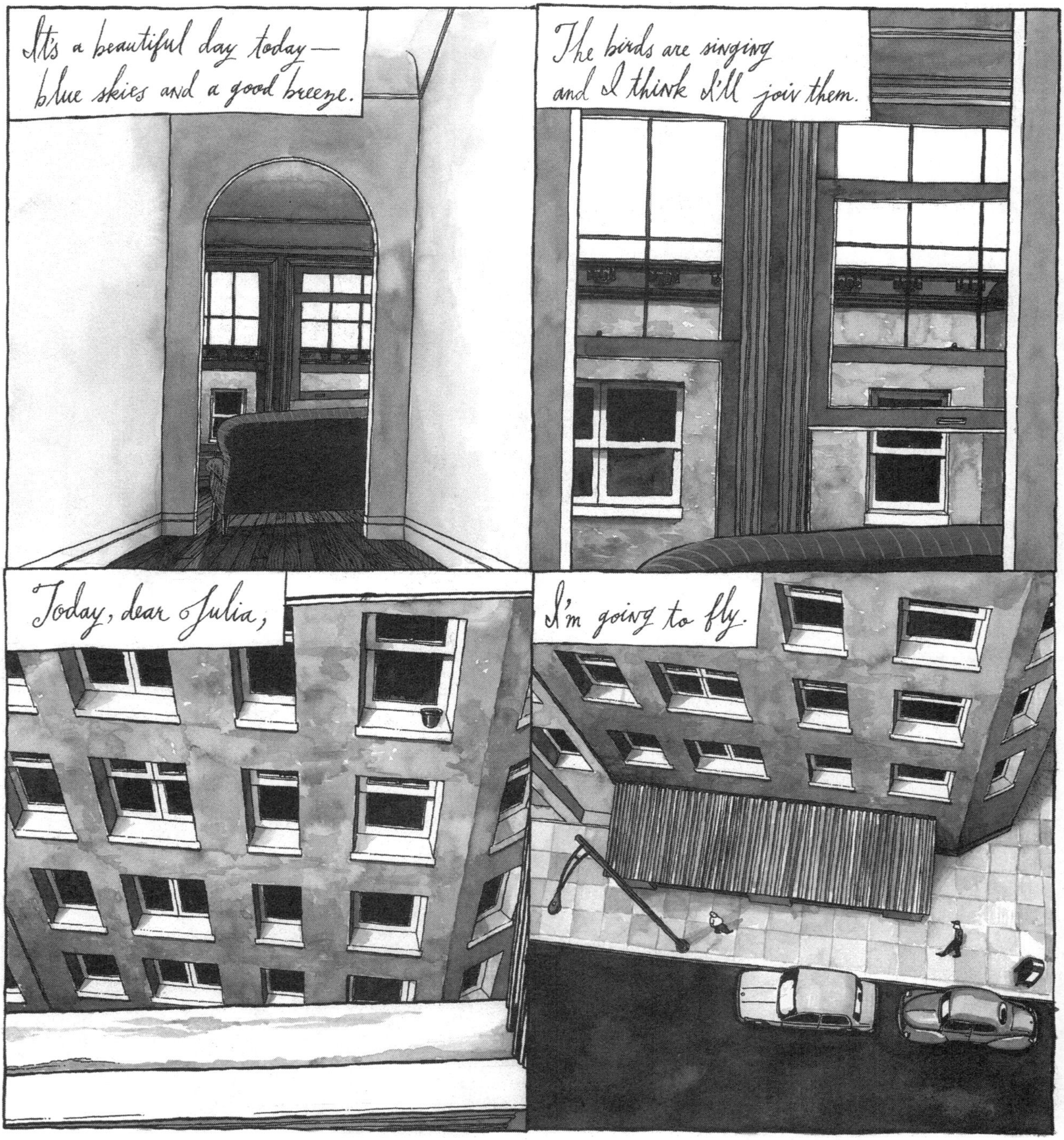
It's a beautiful day today—
blue skies and a good breeze.
The birds are singing
and I think I'll join them.
Today, dear Julia,
I'm going to fly.

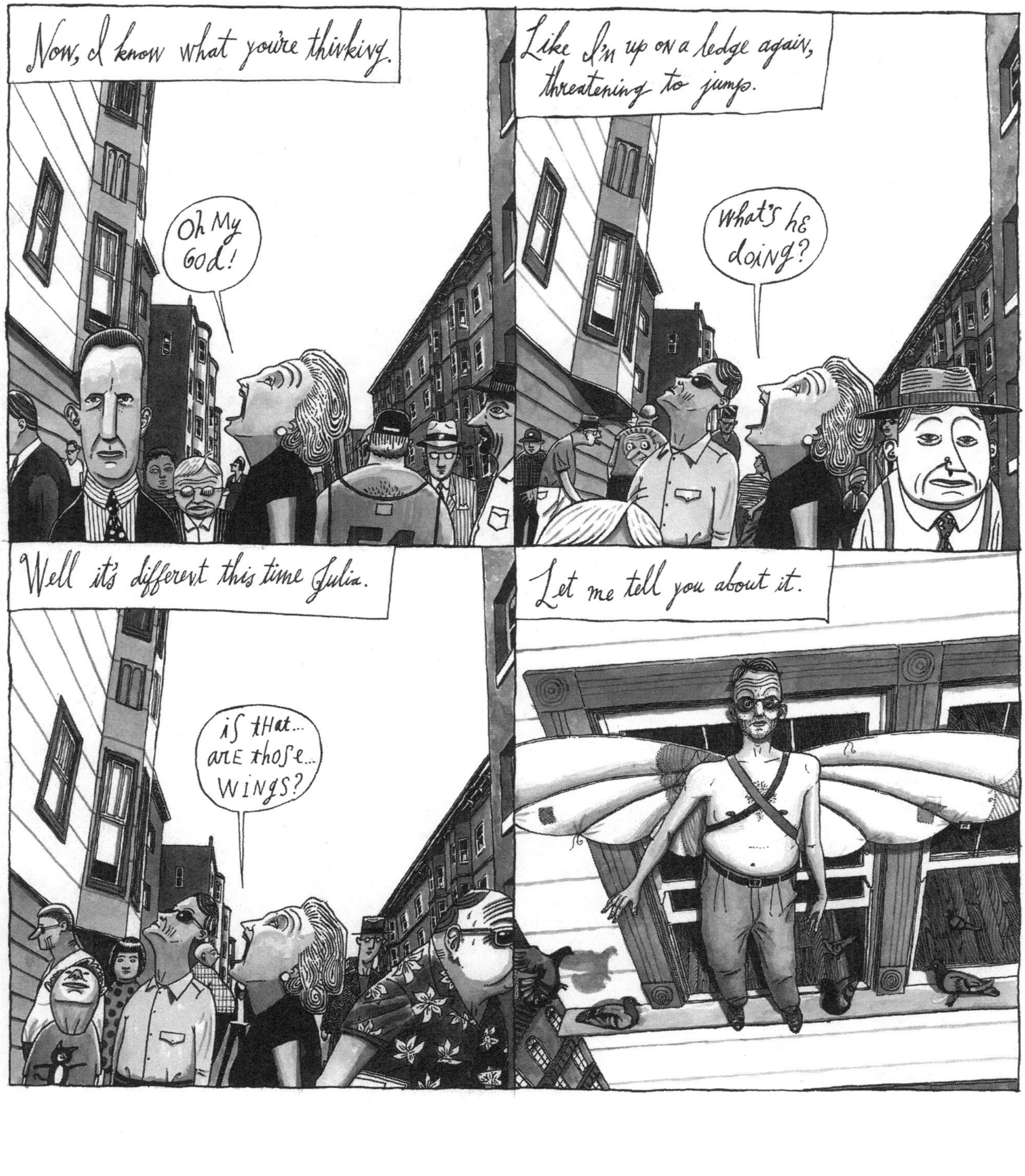
Now, I know what you're thinking.
Oh My God!
Like I'm up on a ledge again, threatening to jump.
What's he doing?
Well it's different this time Julia.
is that... are those... WINGS?
Let me tell you about it.

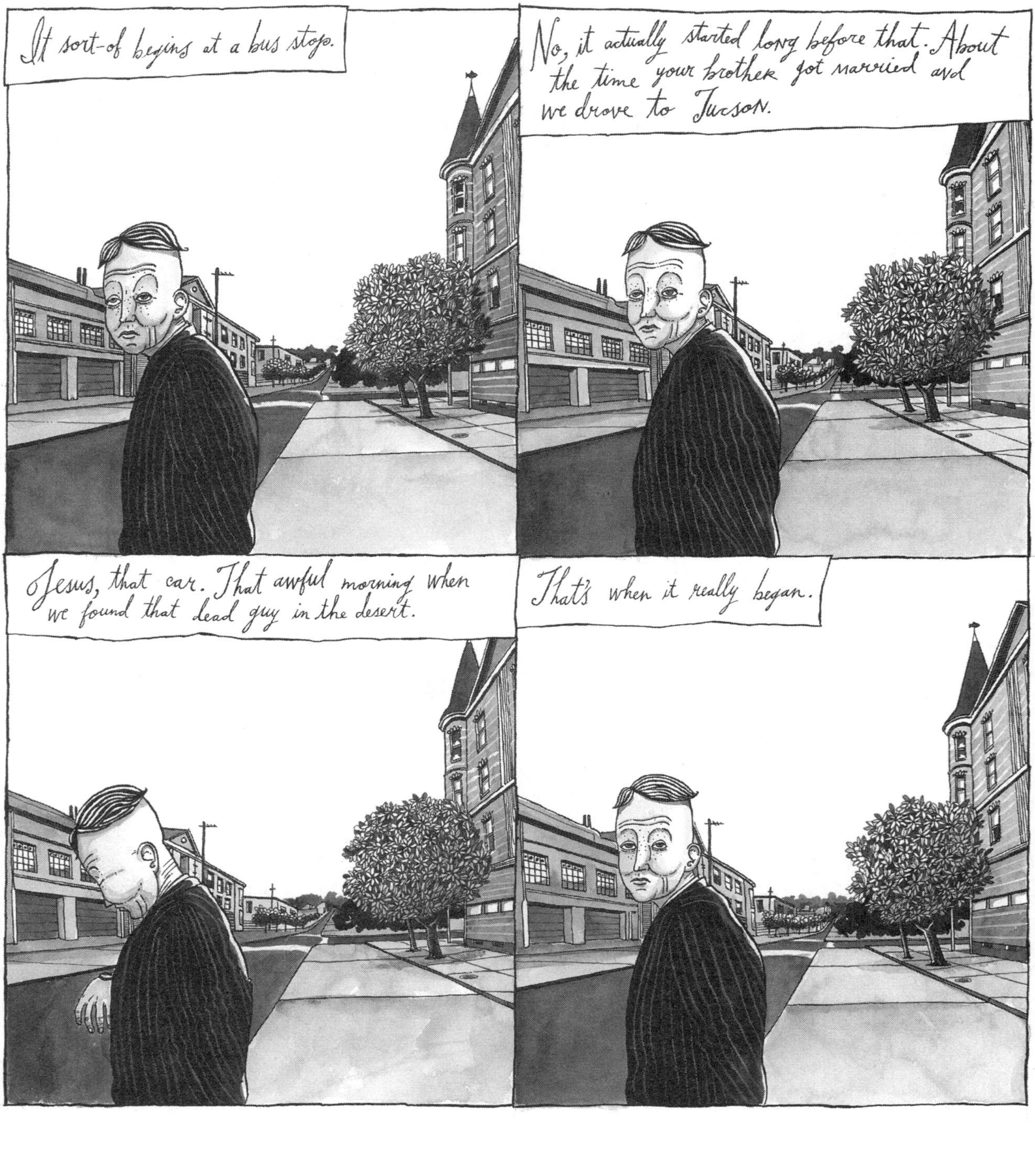
It sort-of begins at a bus stop.
No, it actually started long before that. About the time your brother got married and we drove to Tucson.
Jesus, that car. That awful morning when we found that dead guy in the desert.
That's when it really began.

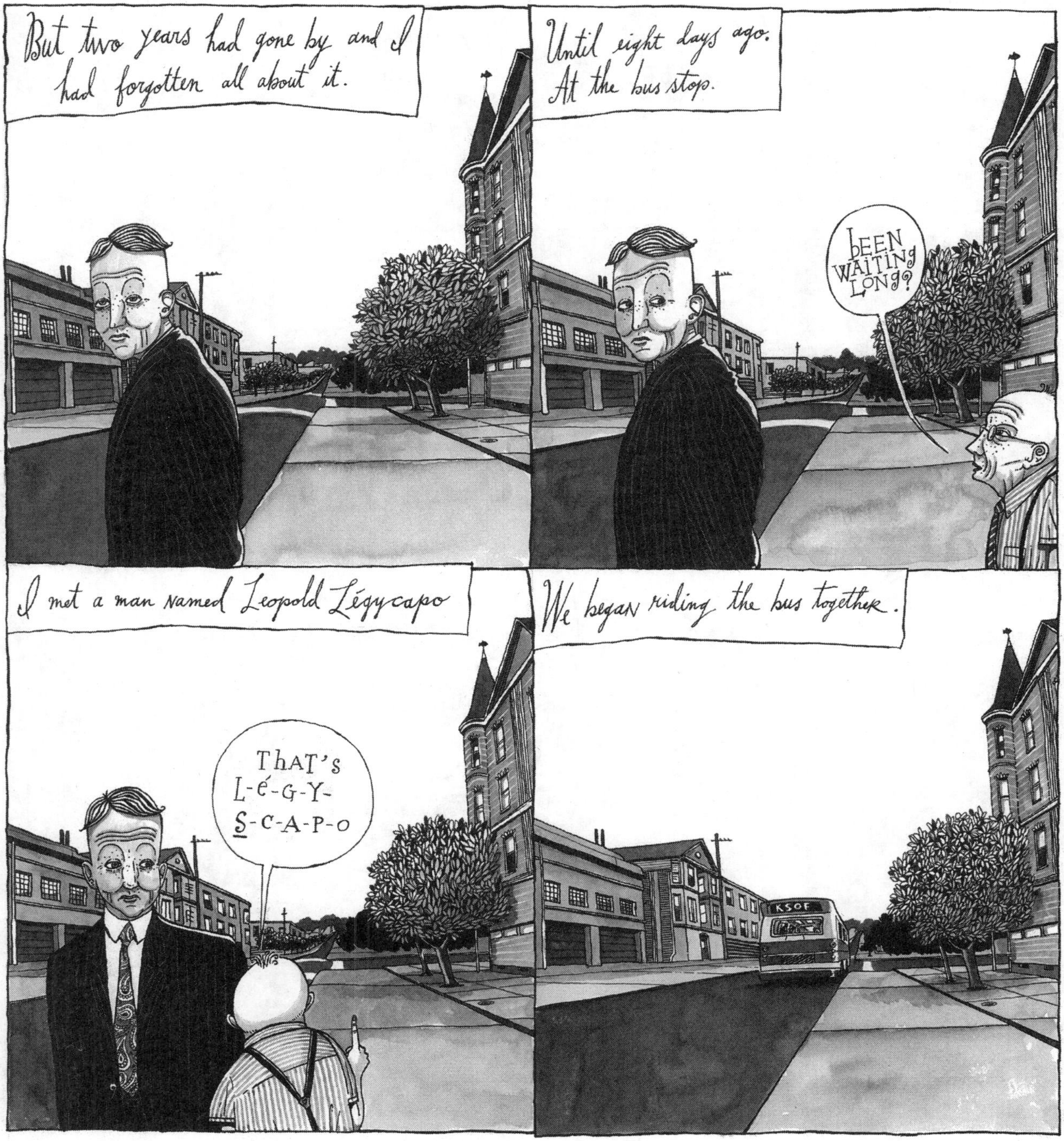
But two years had gone by and I had forgotten all about it.
Until eight days ago. At the bus stop.
BEEN WAITING LONG?
I met a man named Leopold Légycapo
THAT'S L-É-G-Y-S-C-A-P-O
We began riding the bus together.
KSOF

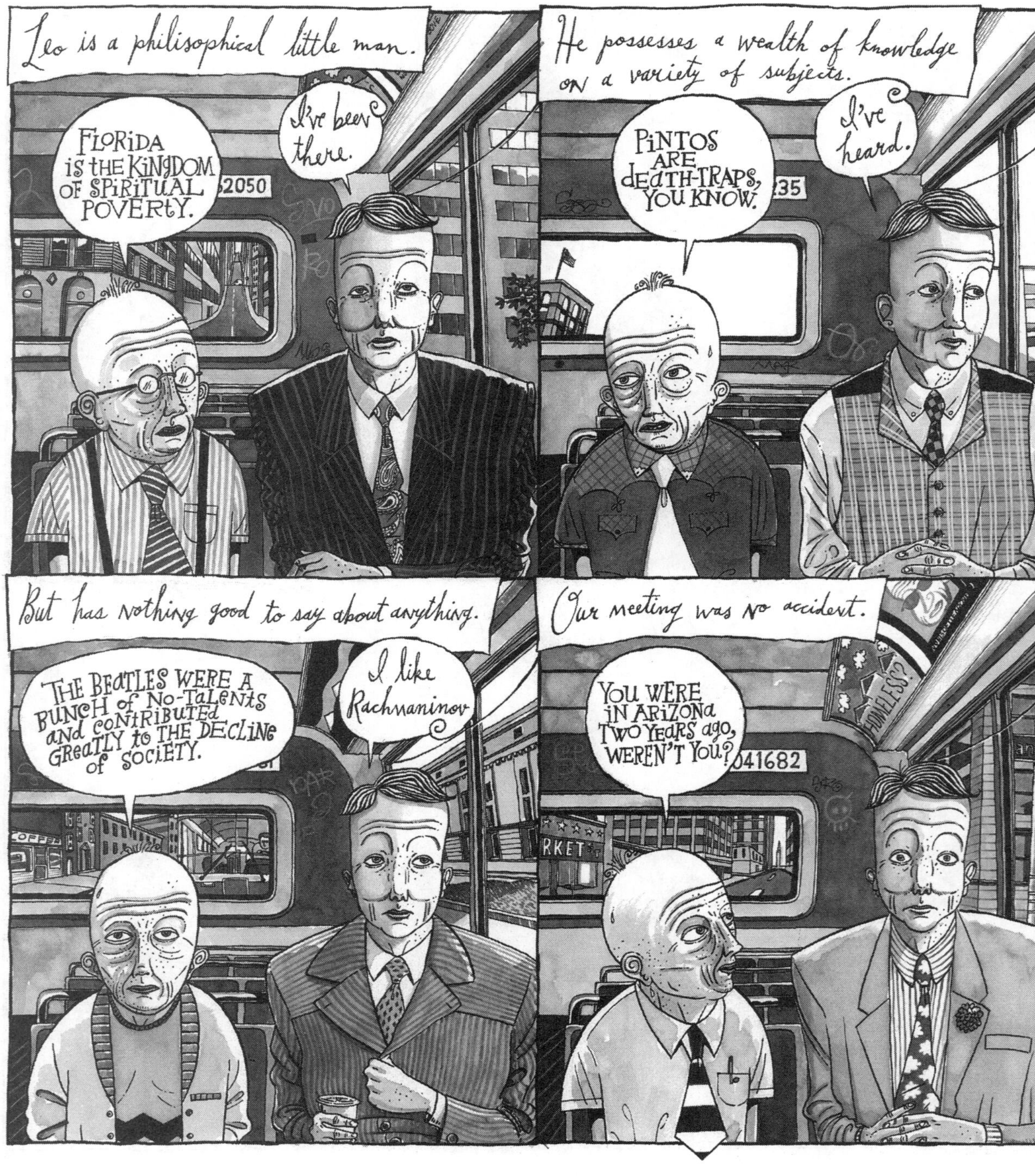
Leo is a philisophical little man.
FLORIDA is the KINGDOM OF SPIRITUAL POVERTY.
I've been there.
He possesses a wealth of knowledge on a variety of subjects.
PINTOS ARE DEATH-TRAPS, YOU KNOW.
I've heard.
But has nothing good to say about anything.
THE BEATLES WERE A BUNCH of No-TALENTS and CONTRIBUTED GREATLY to THE DECLINE of SOCIETY.
I like Rachmaninov
Our meeting was no accident.
YOU WERE IN ARIZONA TWO YEARS ago, WEREN'T YOU?

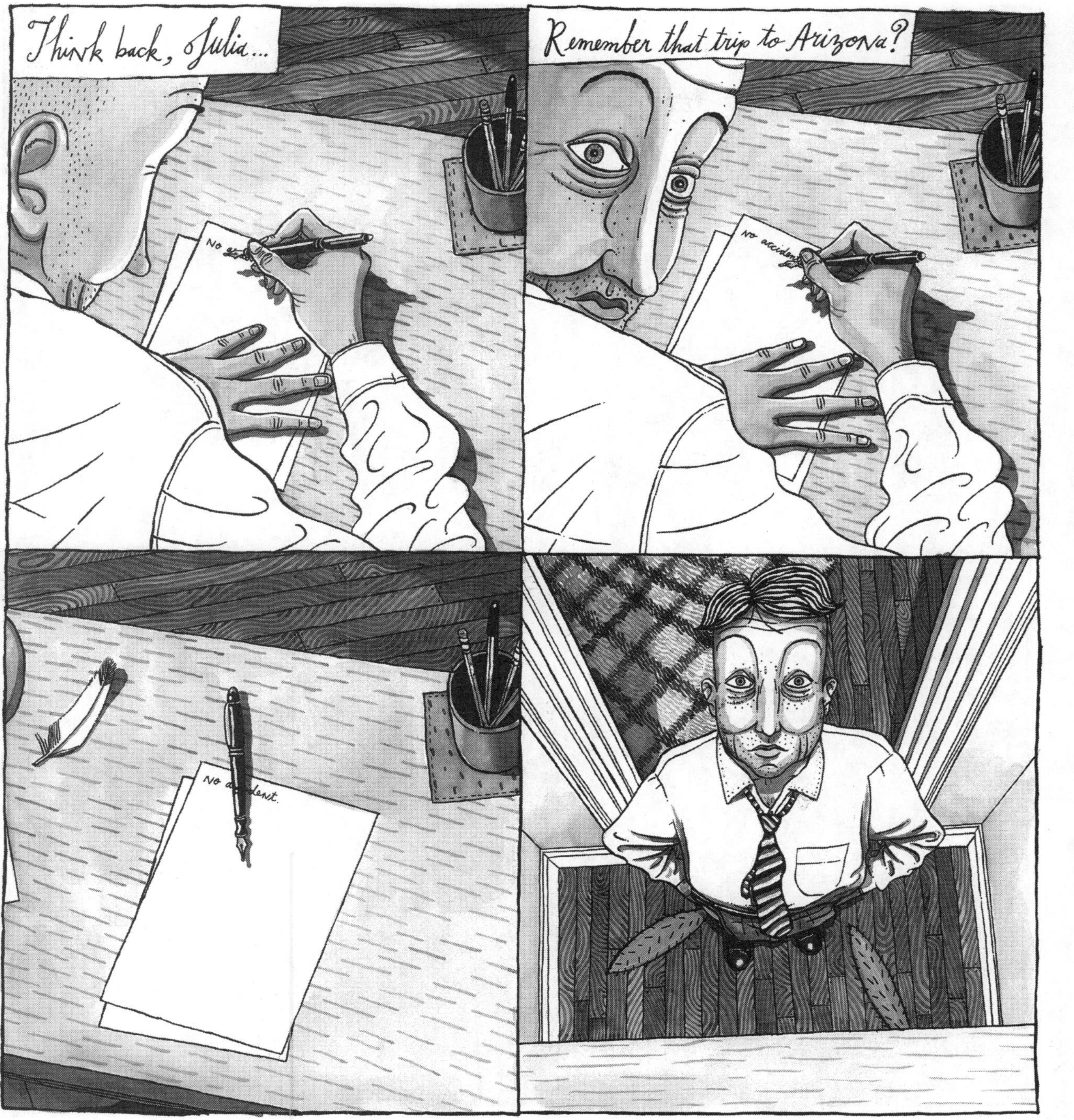
Think back, Julia...
Remember that trip to Arizona?

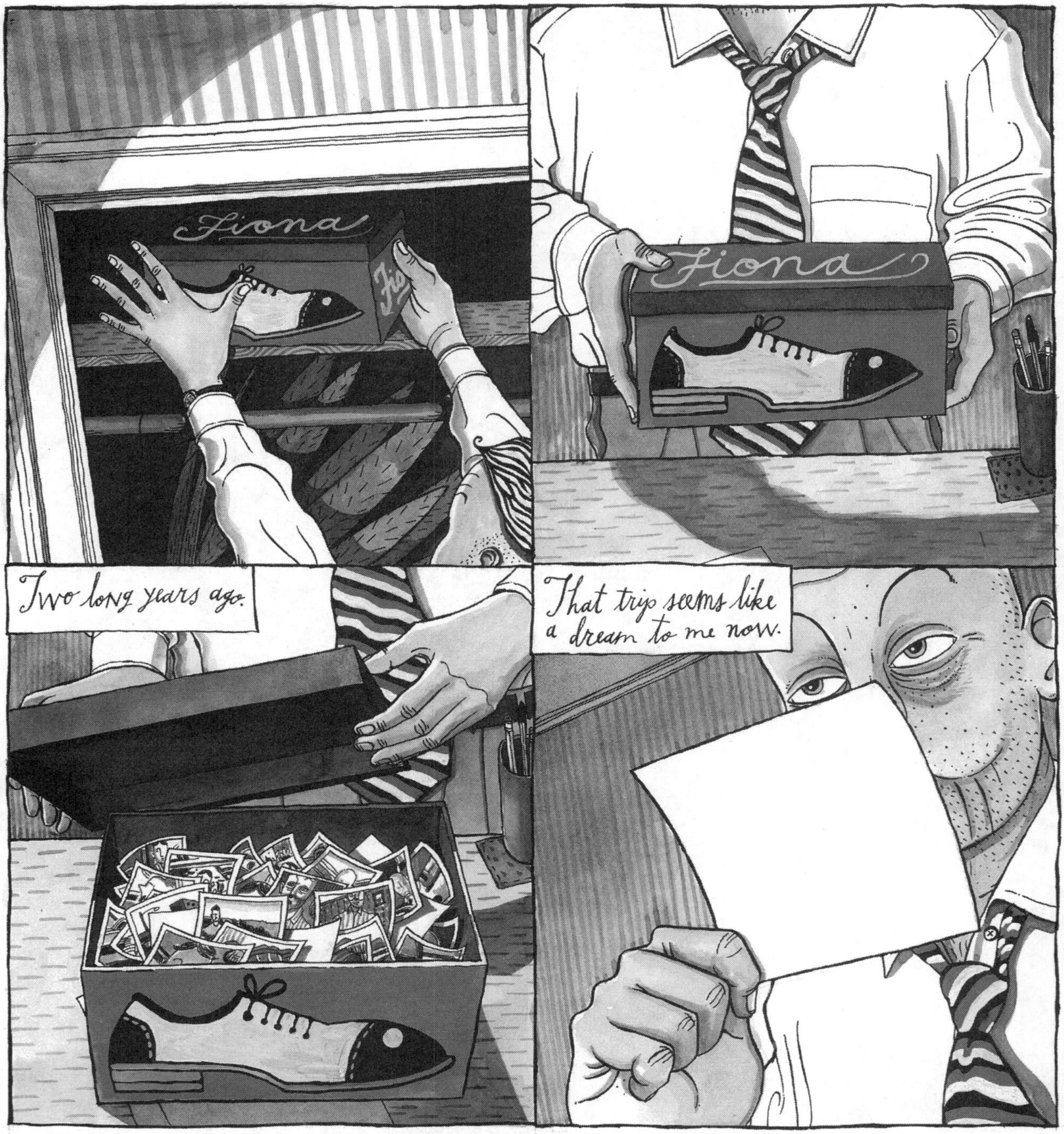
Fiona
Fio
Fiona
Two long years ago.
That trip seems like a dream to me now.
Fiona

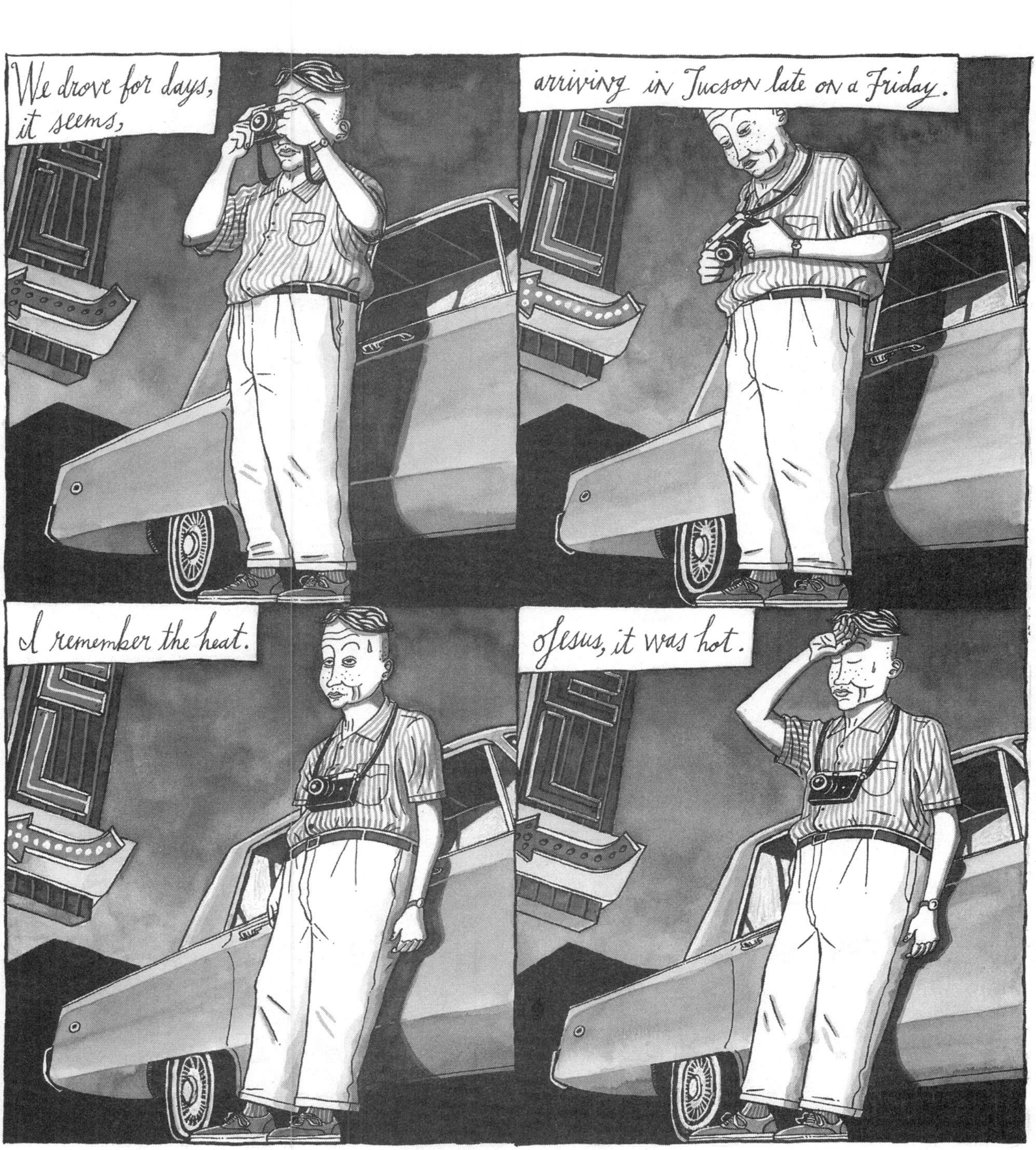
We drove for days, it seems,
arriving in Tucson late on a Friday.
I remember the heat.
Jesus, it was hot.

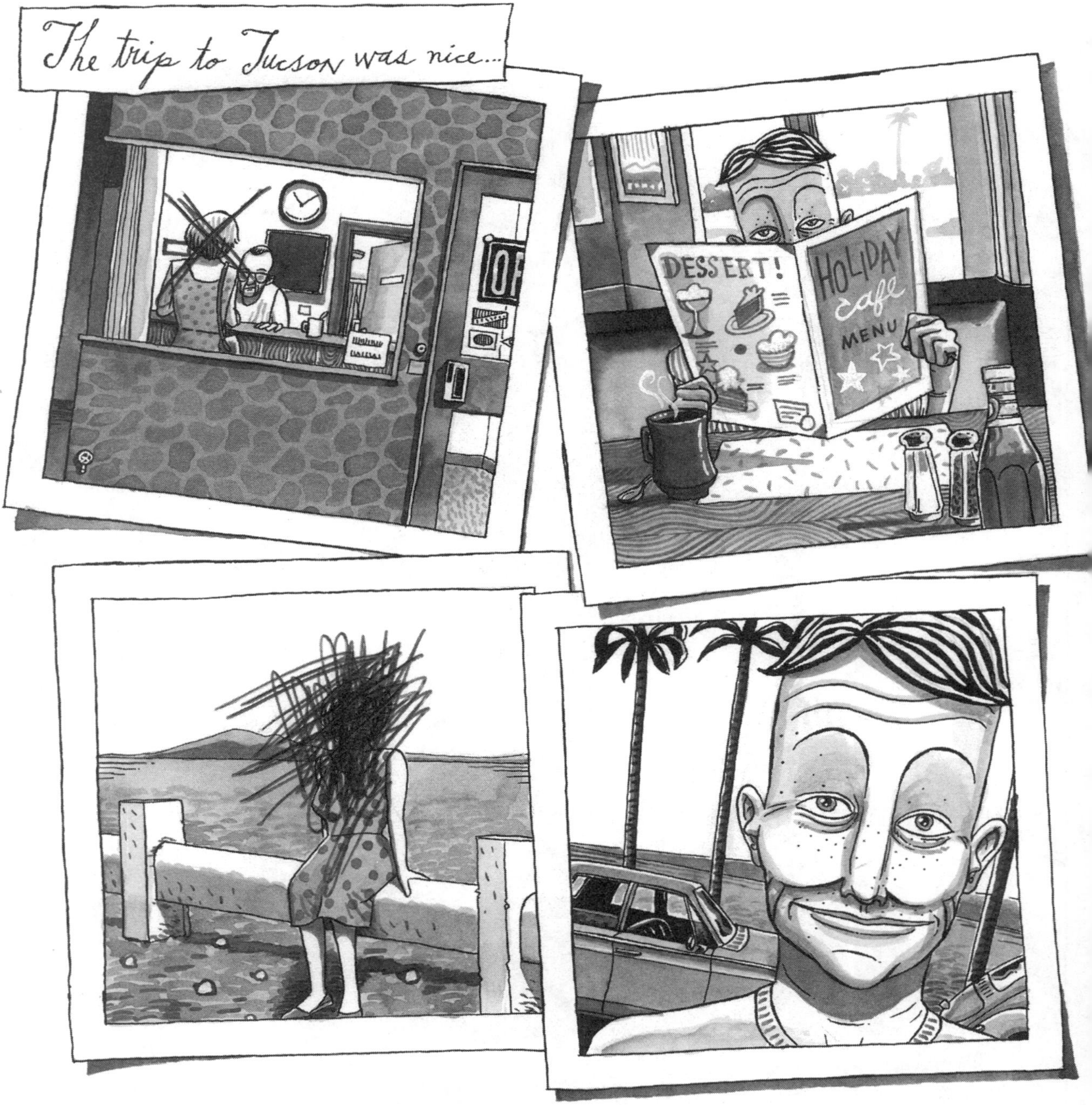
The trip to Tucson was nice...
DESSERT!
HOLIDAY
cafe
MENU

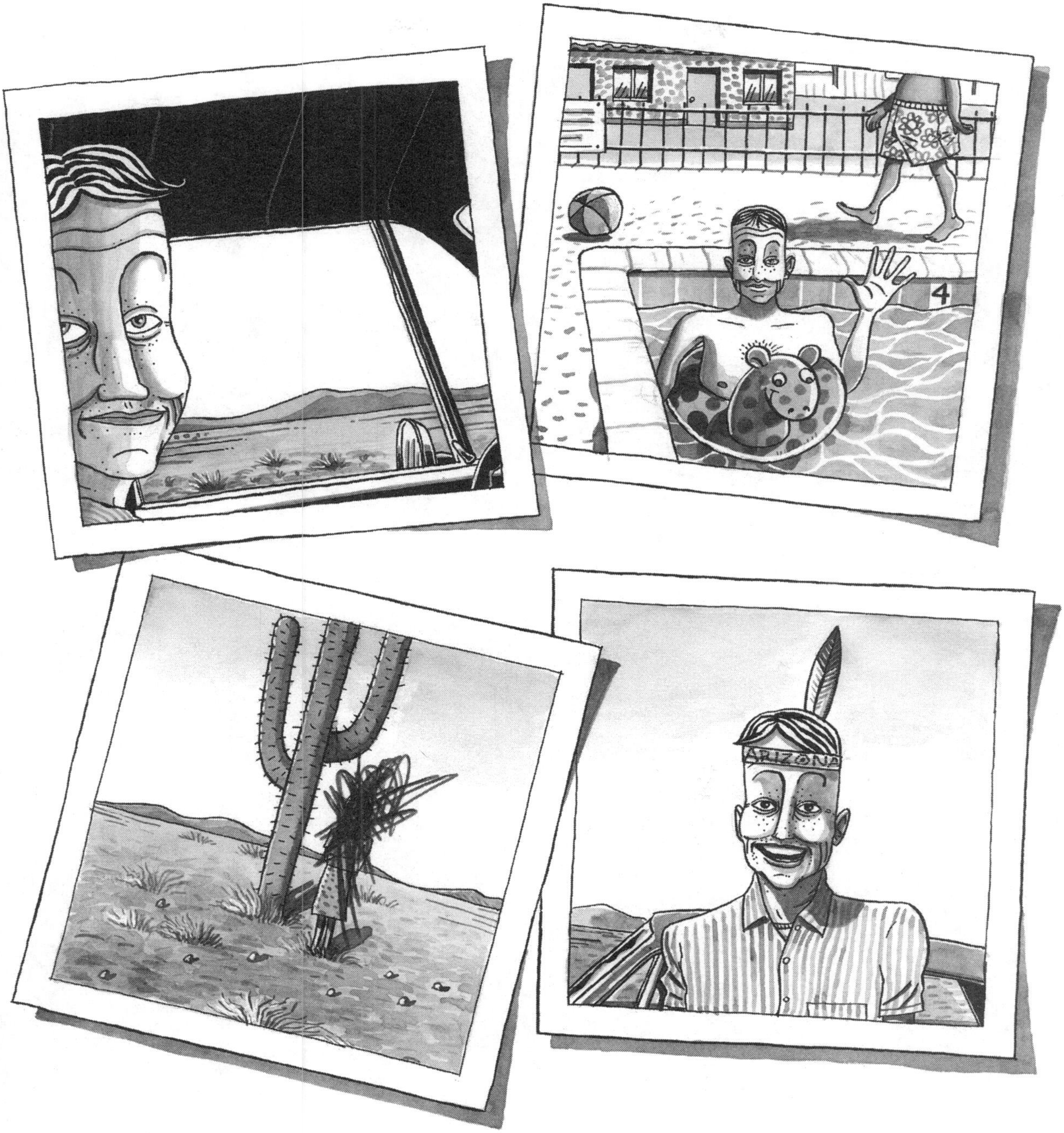
4
ARIZONA

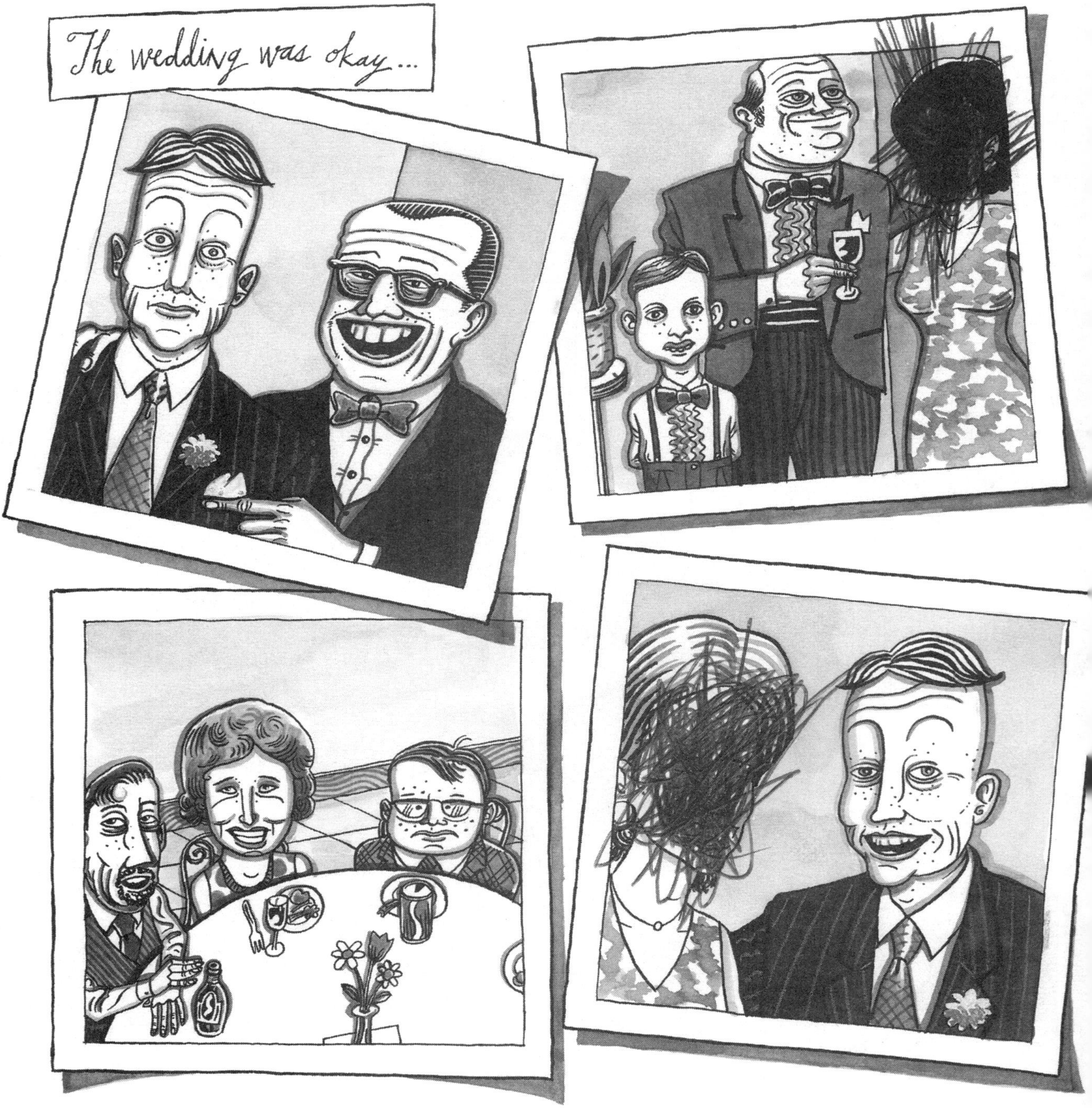
The wedding was okay...

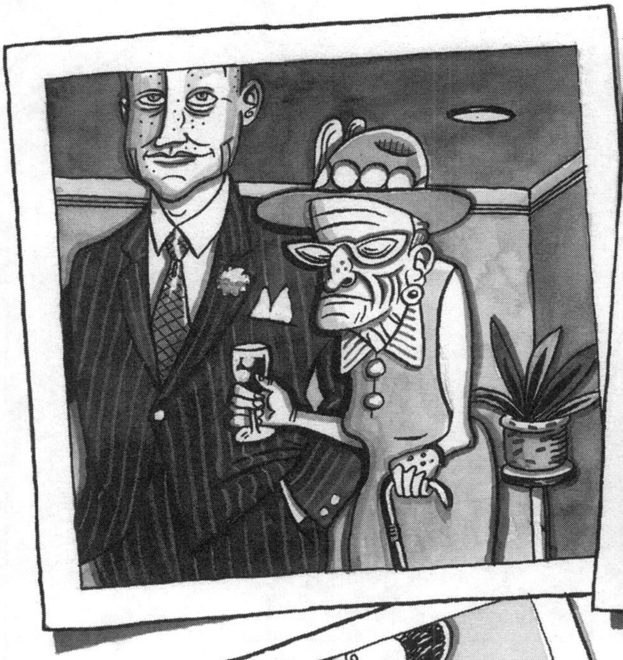

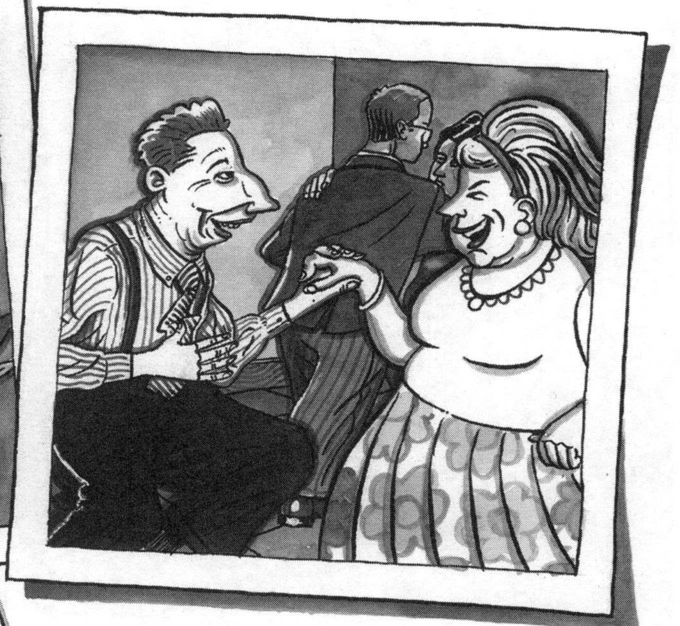

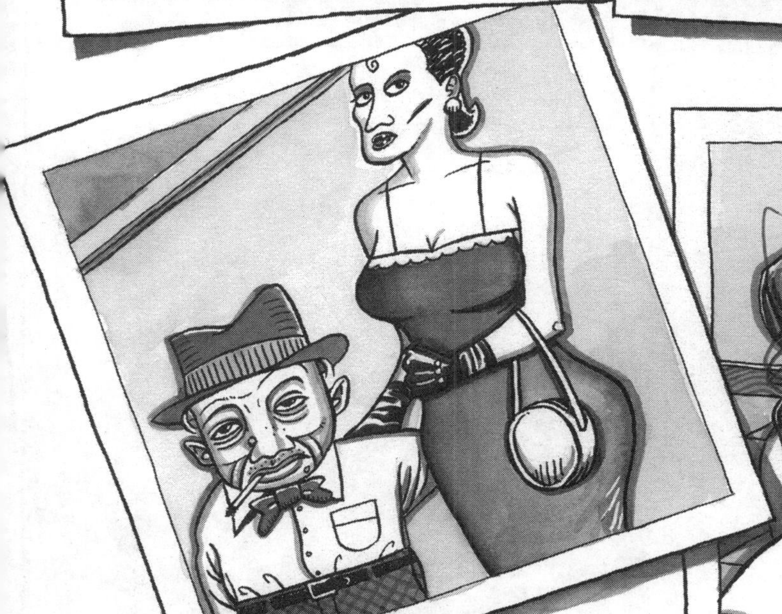

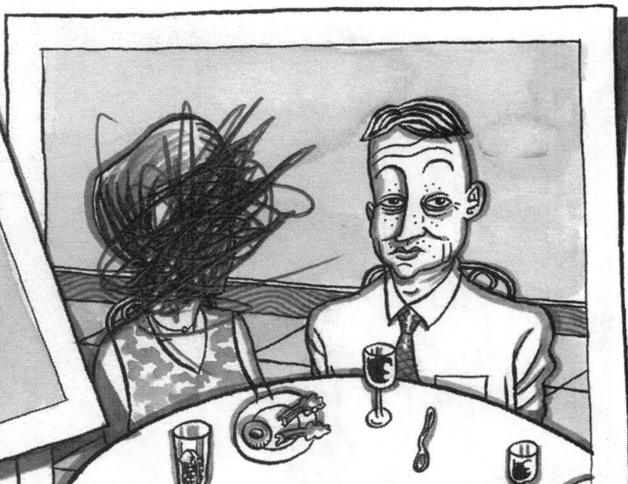

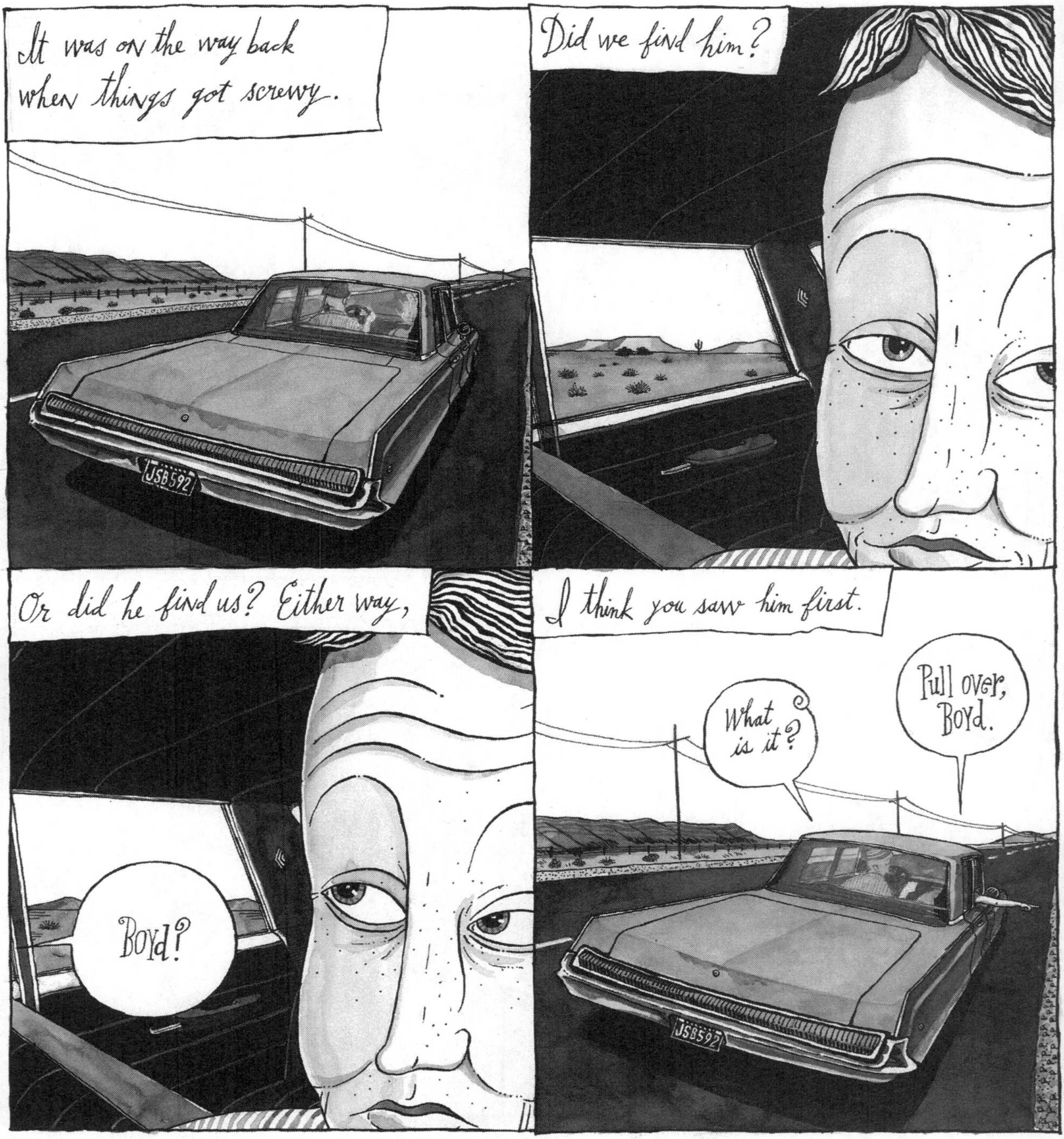
It was on the way back when things got screwy.
Did we find him?
Or did he find us? Either way,
Boyd?
I think you saw him first.
What is it?
Pull over, Boyd.
JSB592

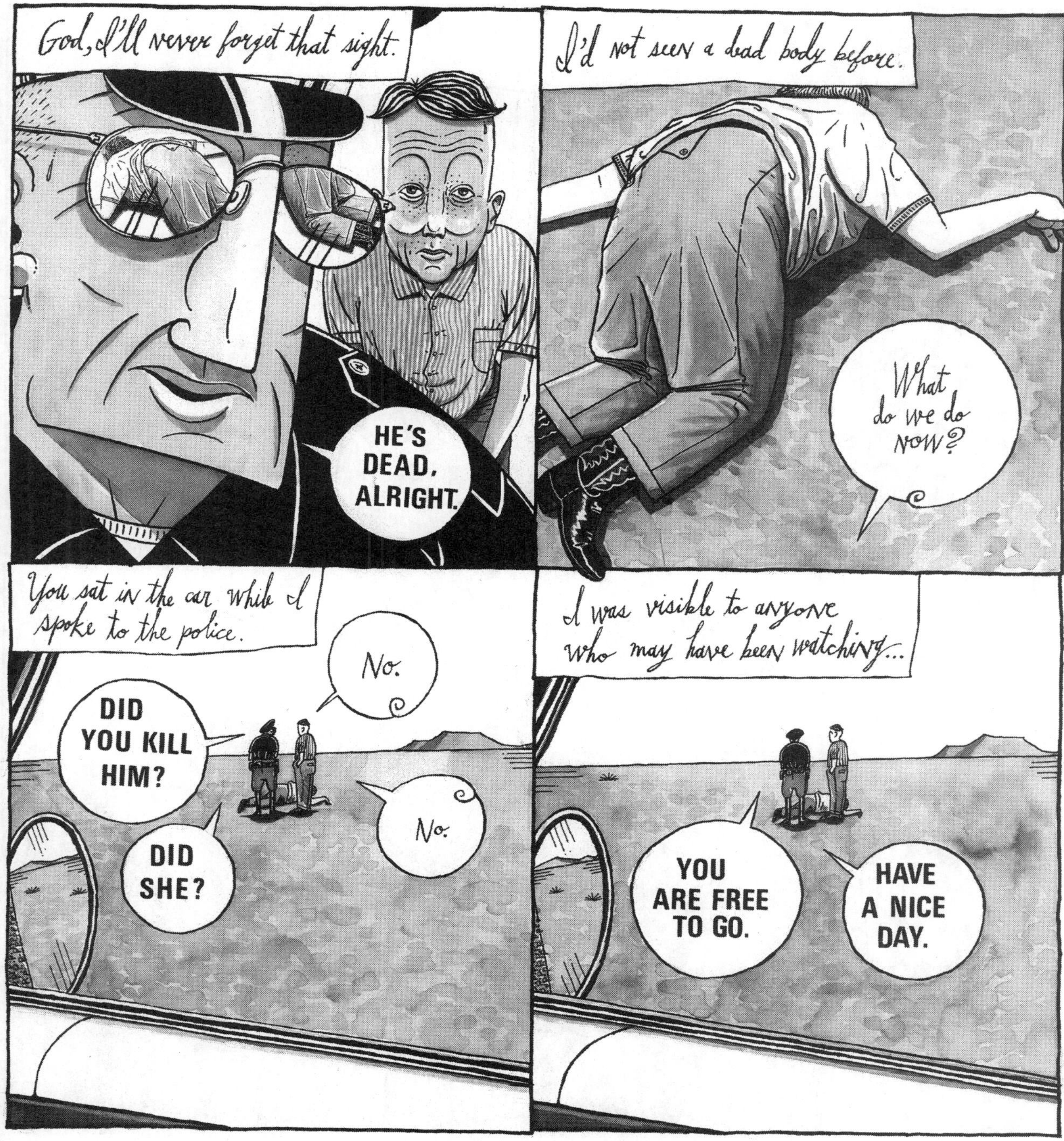
God, I'll never forget that sight.
HE'S DEAD, ALRIGHT.
I'd not seen a dead body before.
What do we do NOW?
You sat in the car while I spoke to the police.
No.
DID YOU KILL HIM?
DID SHE?
No.
I was visible to anyone who may have been watching...
YOU ARE FREE TO GO.
HAVE A NICE DAY.

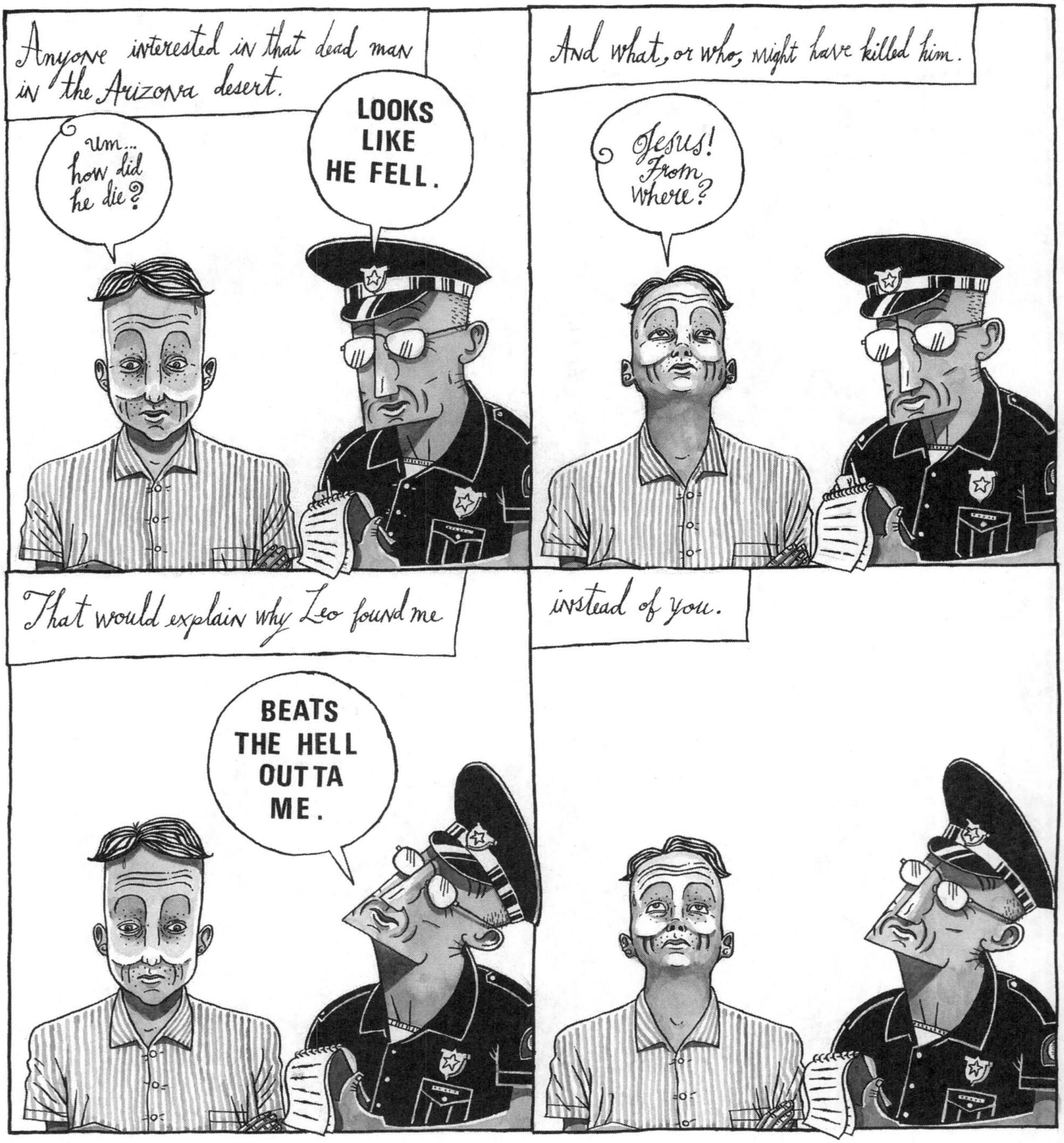
Anyone interested in that dead man in the Arizona desert.
um... how did he die?
LOOKS LIKE HE FELL.
And what, or who, might have killed him.
Jesus! From where?
That would explain why Leo found me
BEATS THE HELL OUTTA ME.
instead of you.

TWO

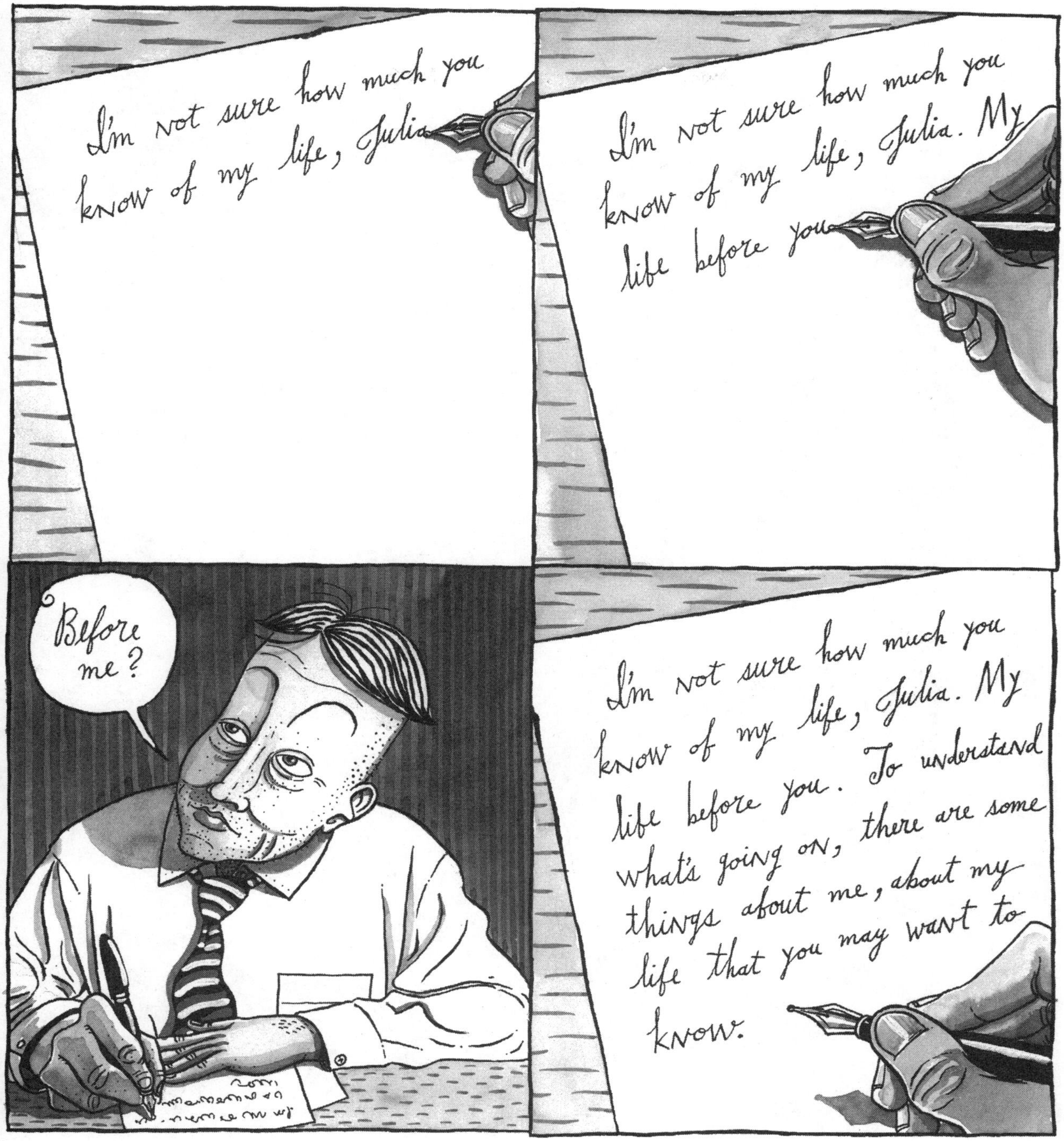
I'm not sure how much you
know of my life, Julia
I'm not sure how much you
know of my life, Julia. My
life before you
Before me?
I'm not sure how much you
know of my life, Julia. My
life before you. To understand
what's going on, there are some
things about me, about my
life that you may want to
know.

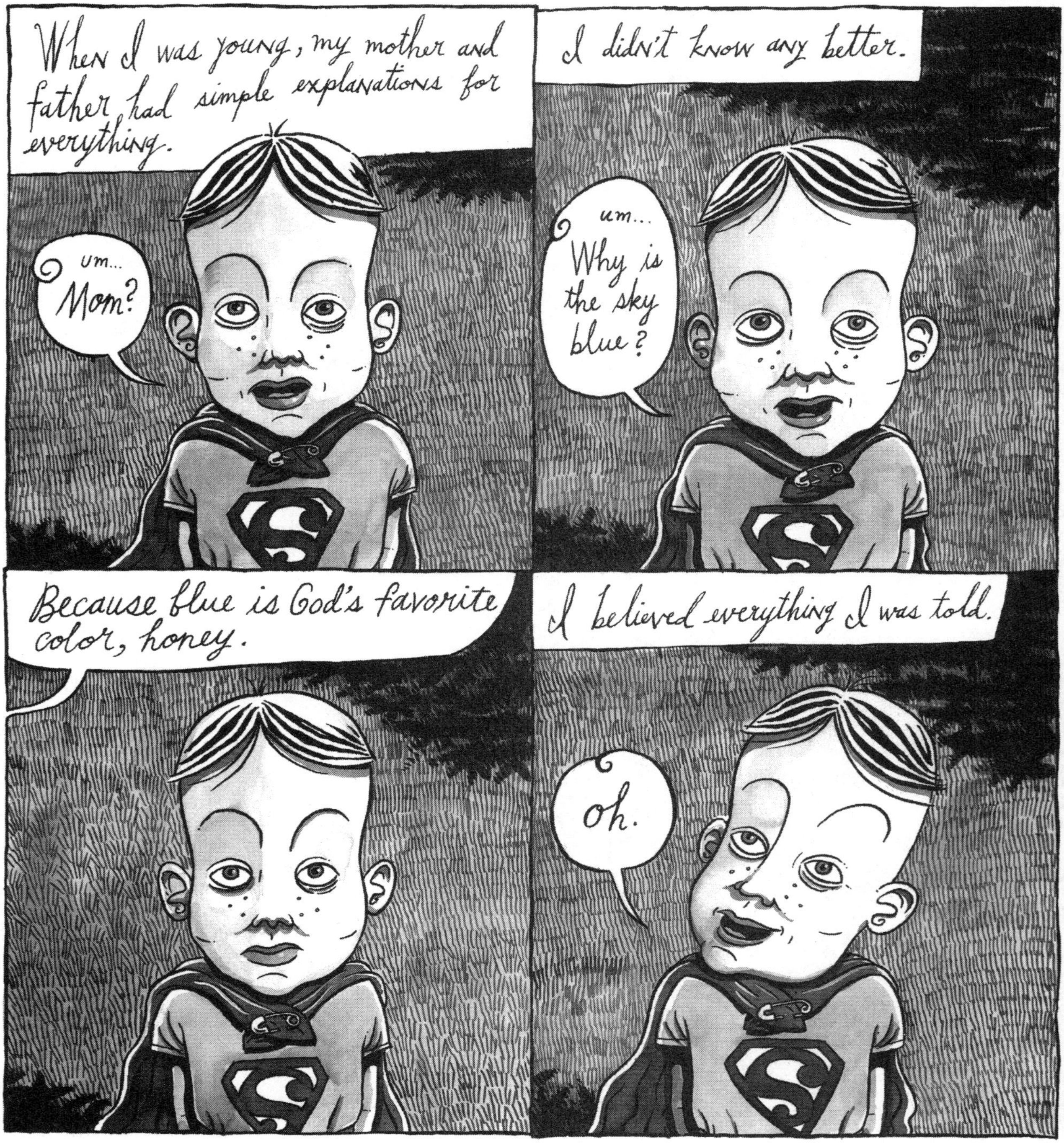
When I was young, my mother and father had simple explanations for everything.
um... Mom?
I didn't know any better.
um... Why is the sky blue?
Because blue is God's favorite color, honey.
I believed everything I was told.
oh.

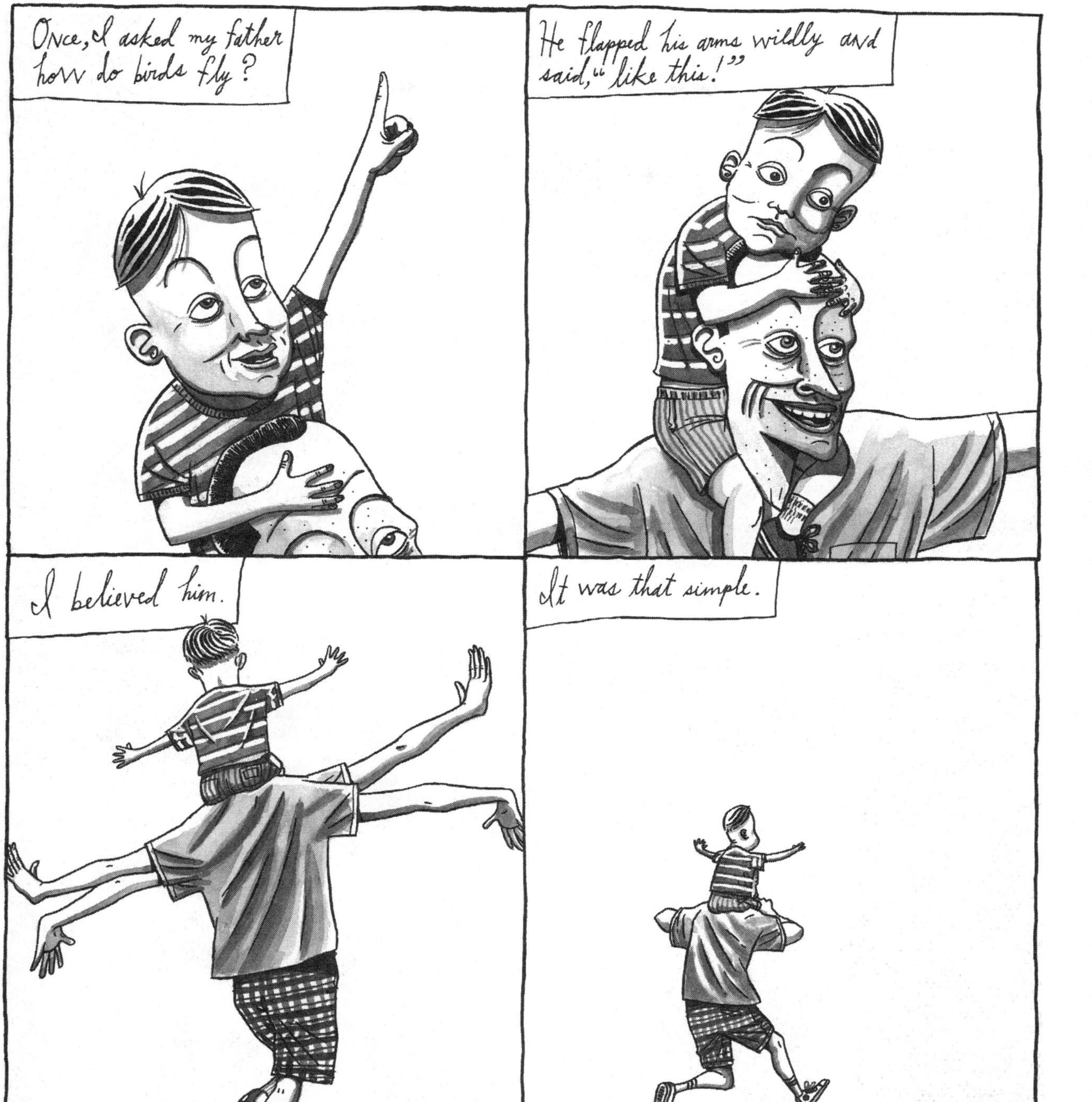
Once, I asked my father how do birds fly?
He flapped his arms wildly and said, "like this!"
I believed him.
It was that simple.

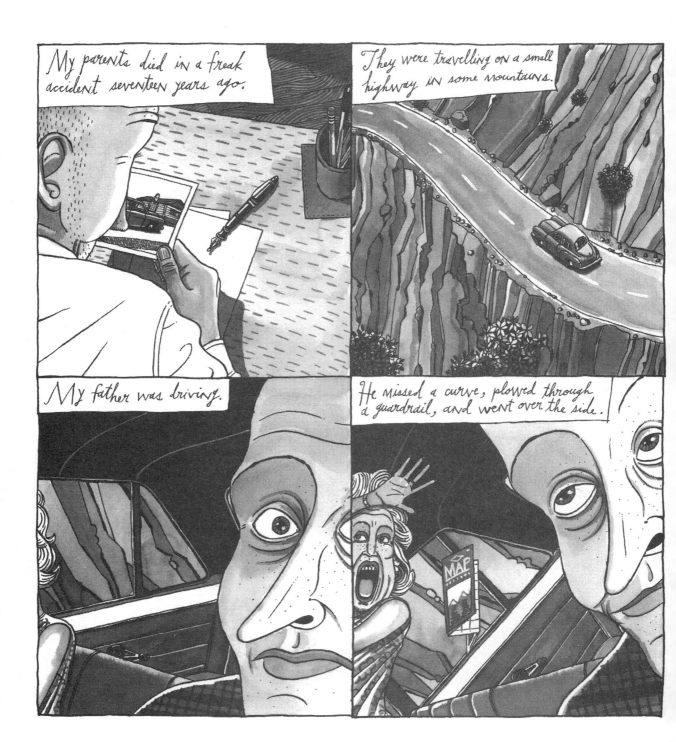

My parents died in a freak accident seventeen years ago.

They were travelling on a small highway in some mountains.

My father was driving.

He missed a curve, plowed through a guardrail, and went over the side.

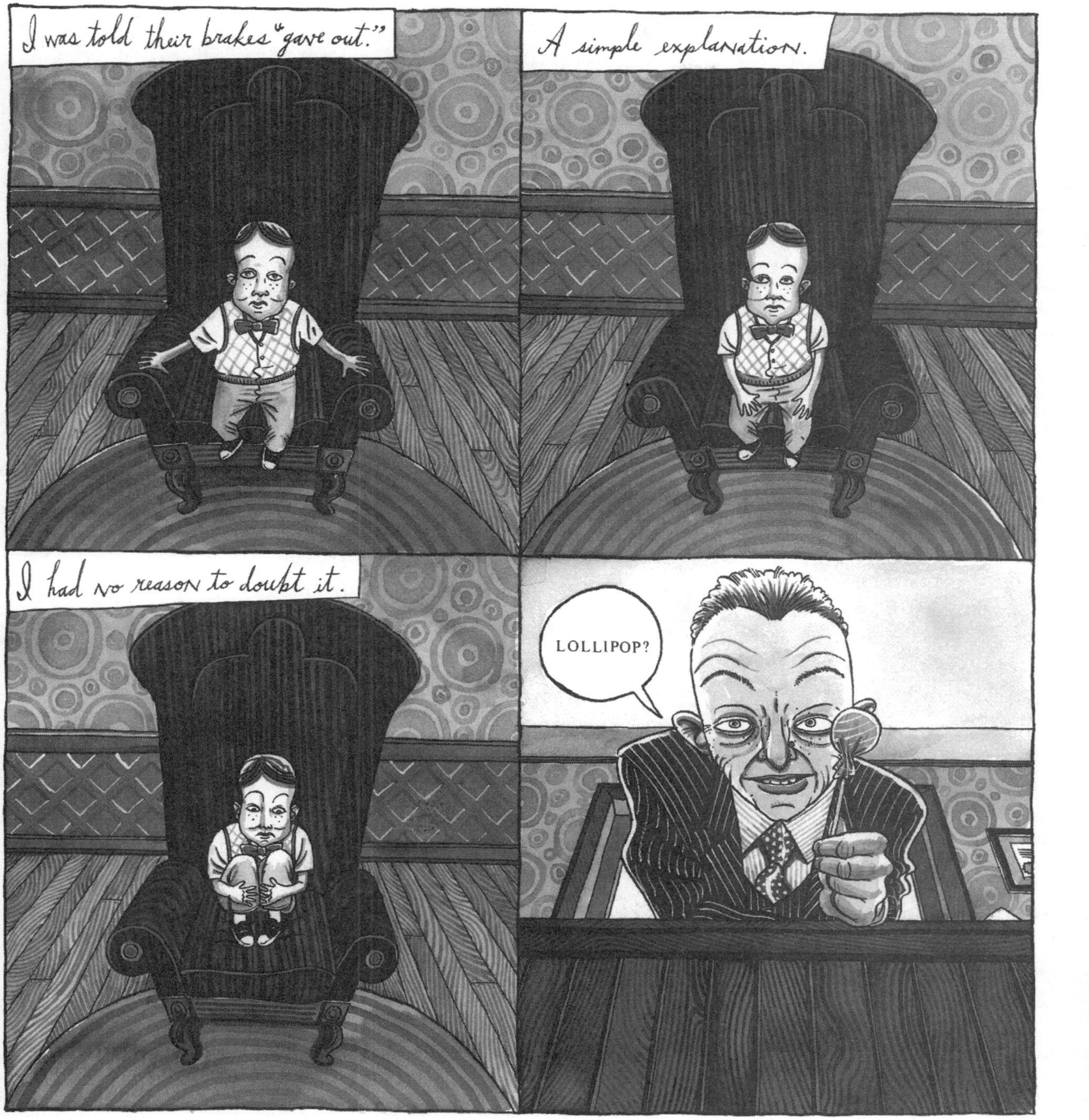
I was told their brakes "gave out."
A simple explanation.
I had no reason to doubt it.
LOLLIPOP?

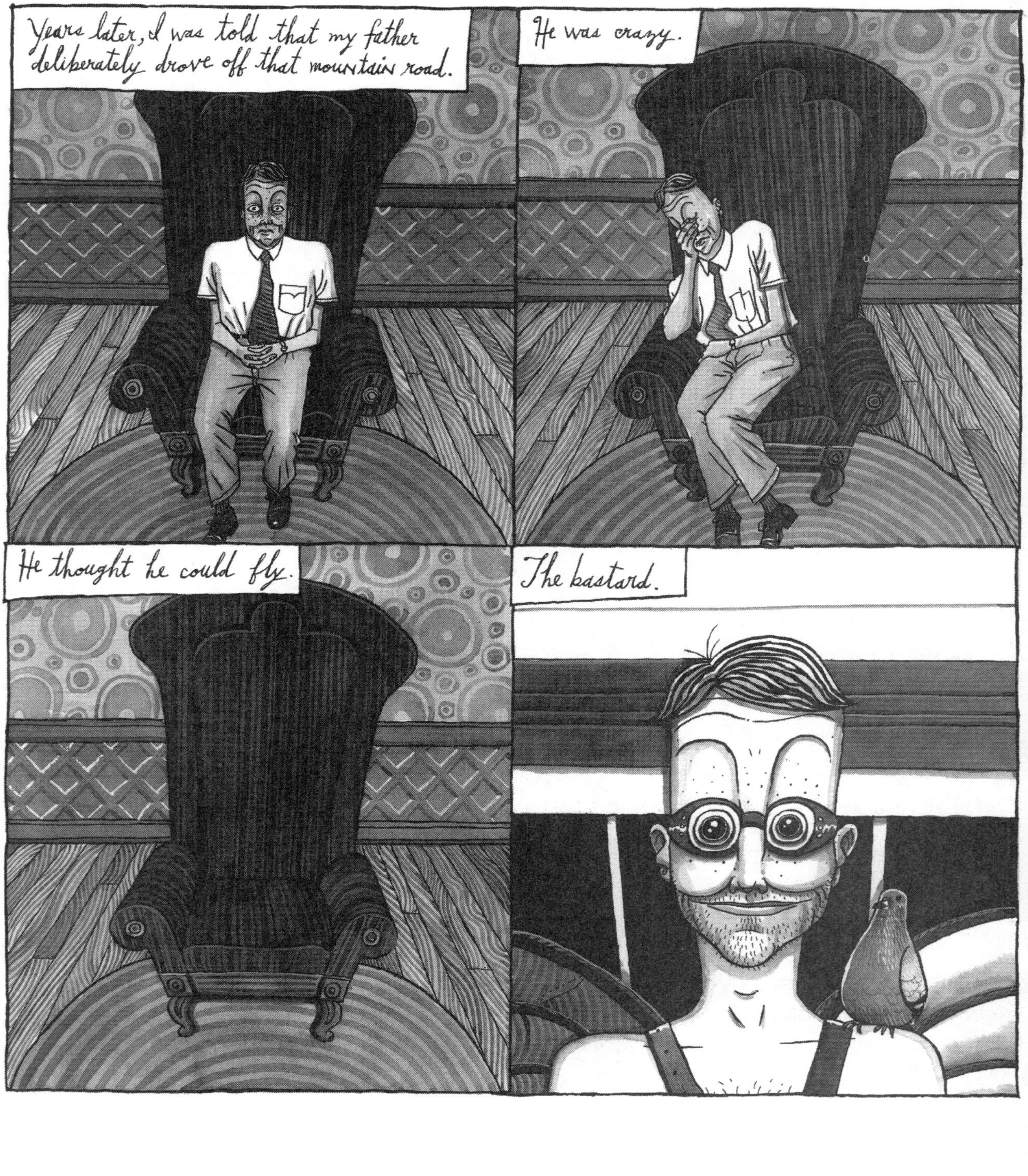
Years later, I was told that my father deliberately drove off that mountain road.
He was crazy.
He thought he could fly.
The bastard.

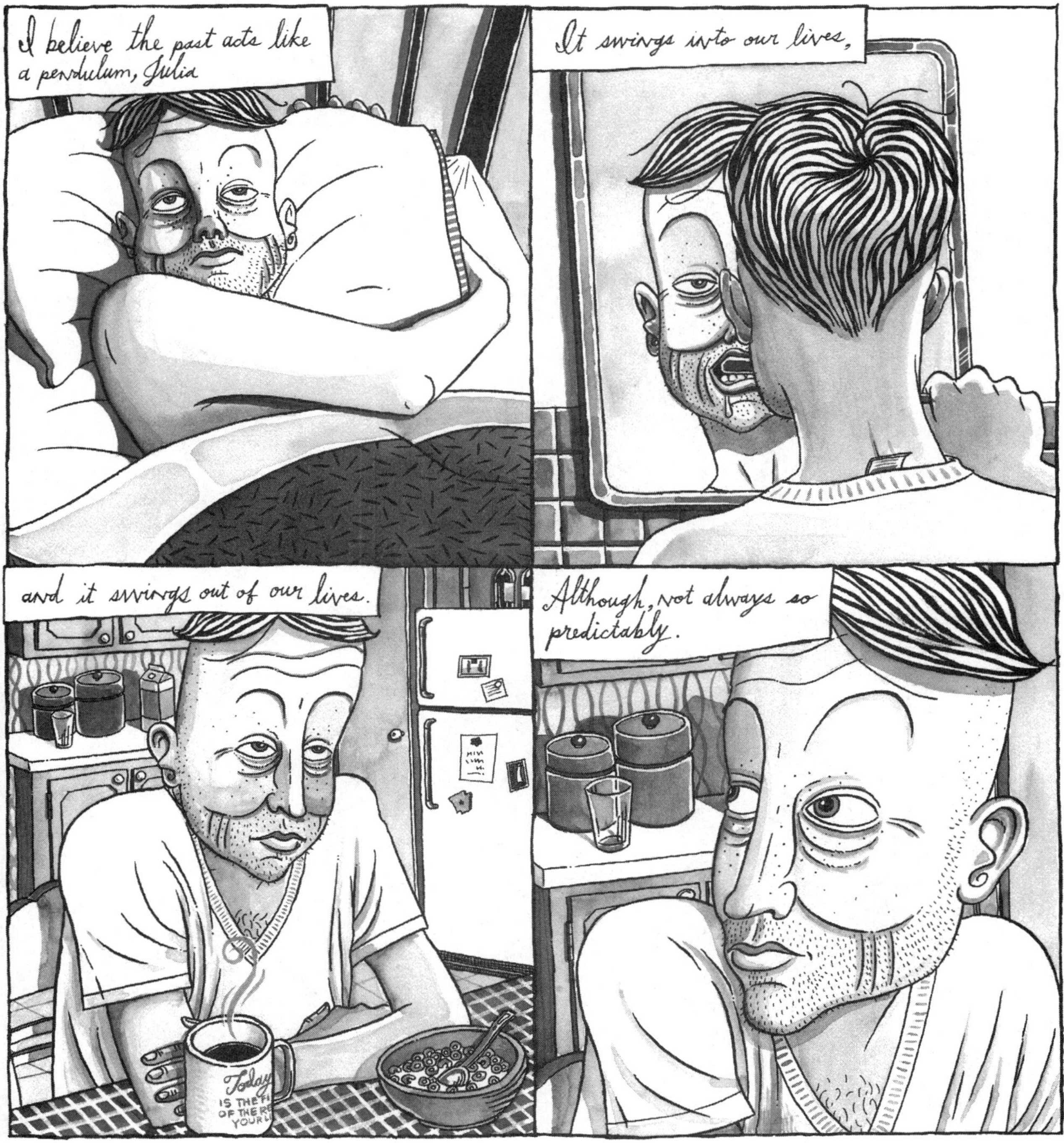
I believe the past acts like a pendulum, Julia
It swings into our lives,
and it swings out of our lives.
Although, not always so predictably.

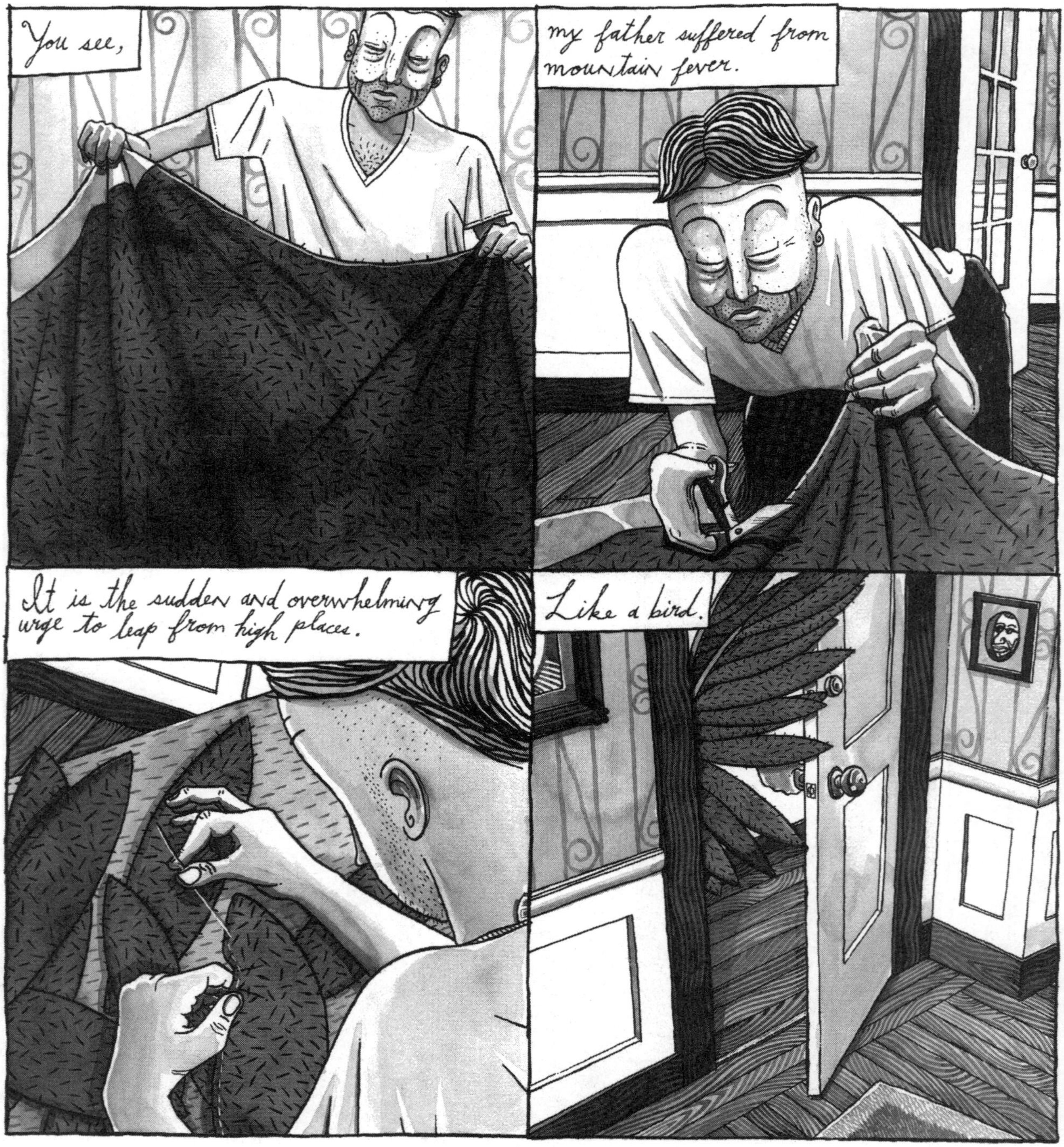
You see,
my father suffered from mountain fever.
It is the sudden and overwhelming urge to leap from high places.
Like a bird.

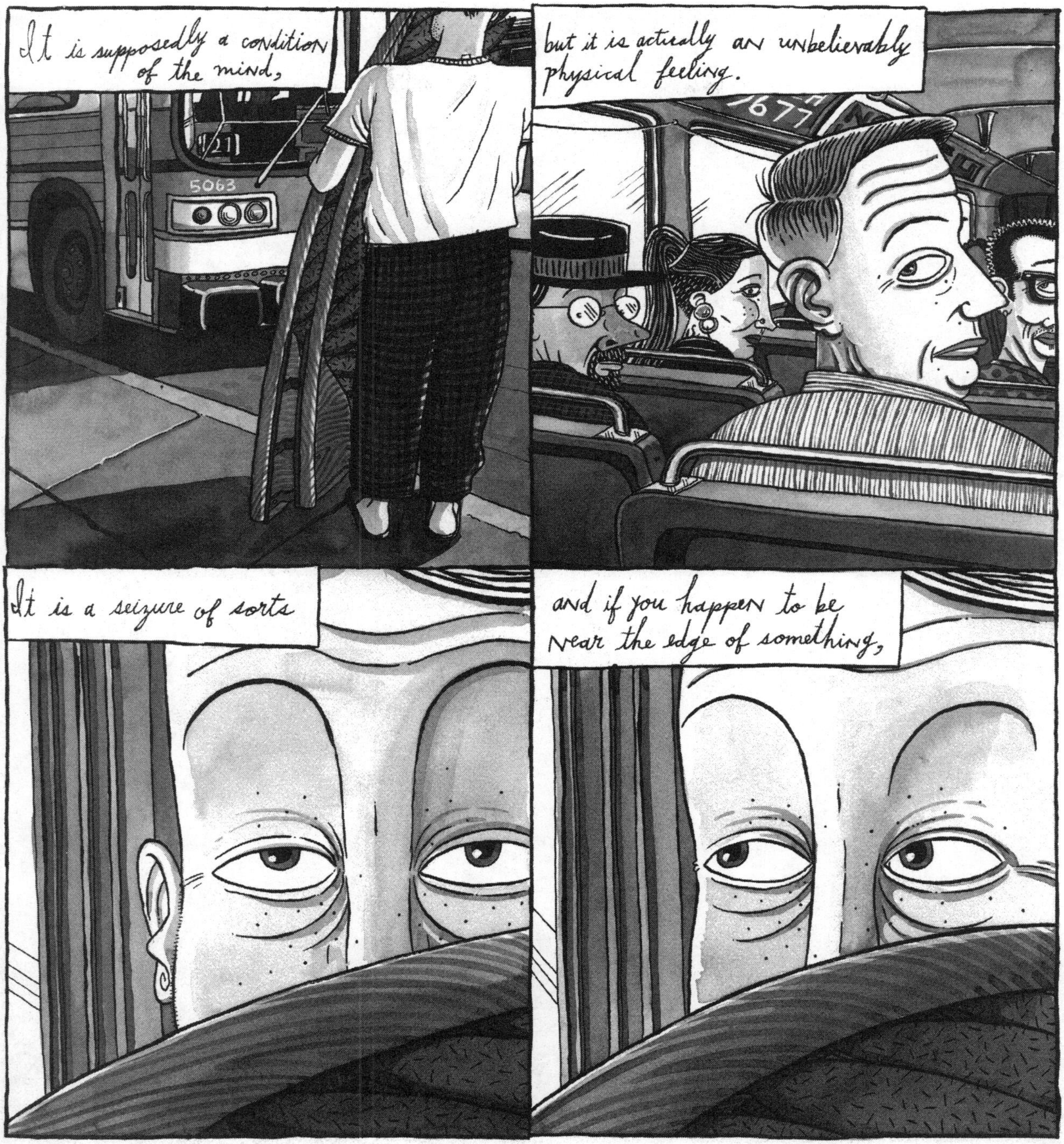
It is supposedly a condition of the mind,
5063
but it is actually an unbelievably physical feeling.
It is a seizure of sorts
and if you happen to be near the edge of something,

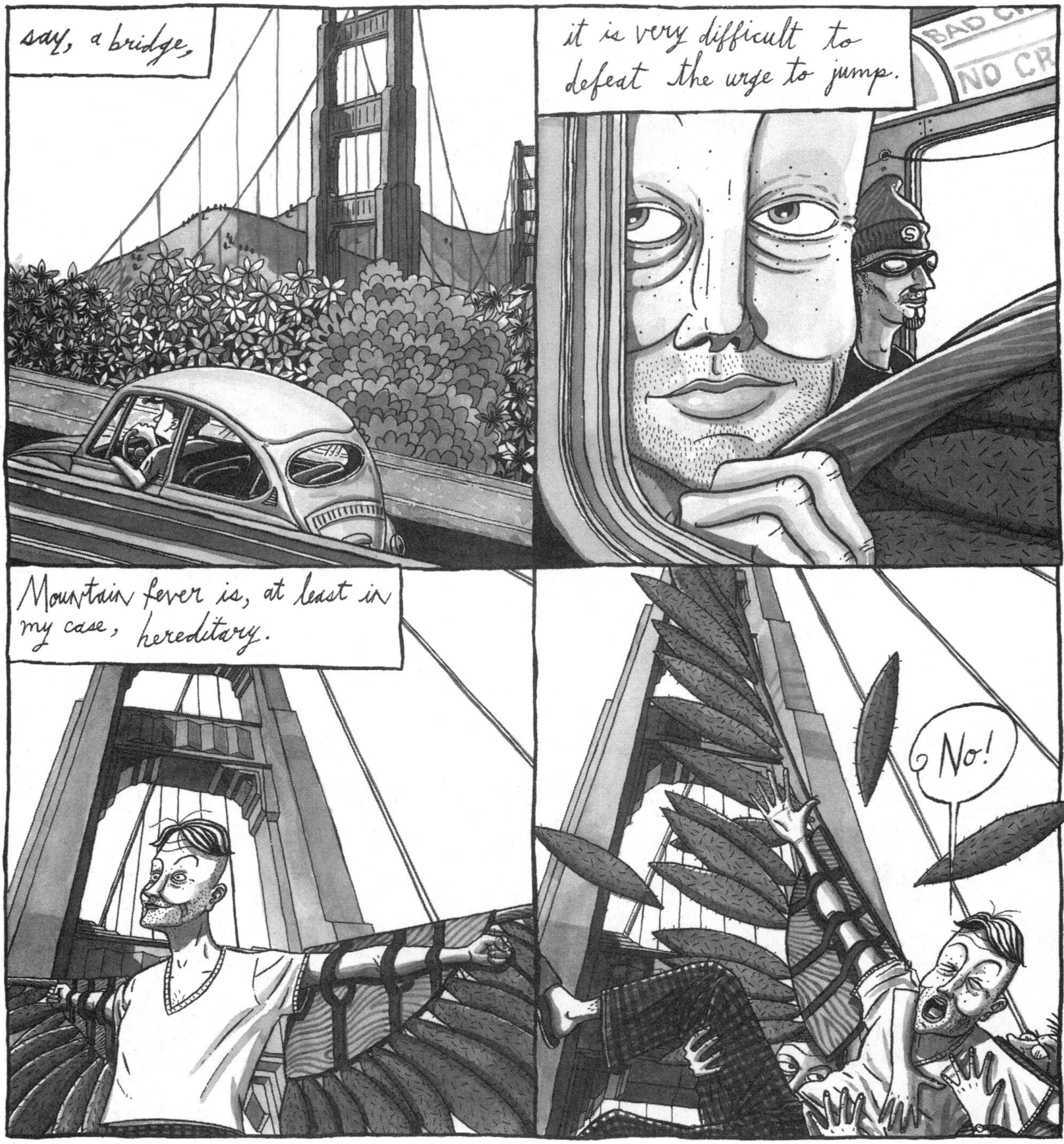
say, a bridge,
it is very difficult to defeat the urge to jump.
BAD C
NO CR
Mountain fever is, at least in my case, hereditary.
No!

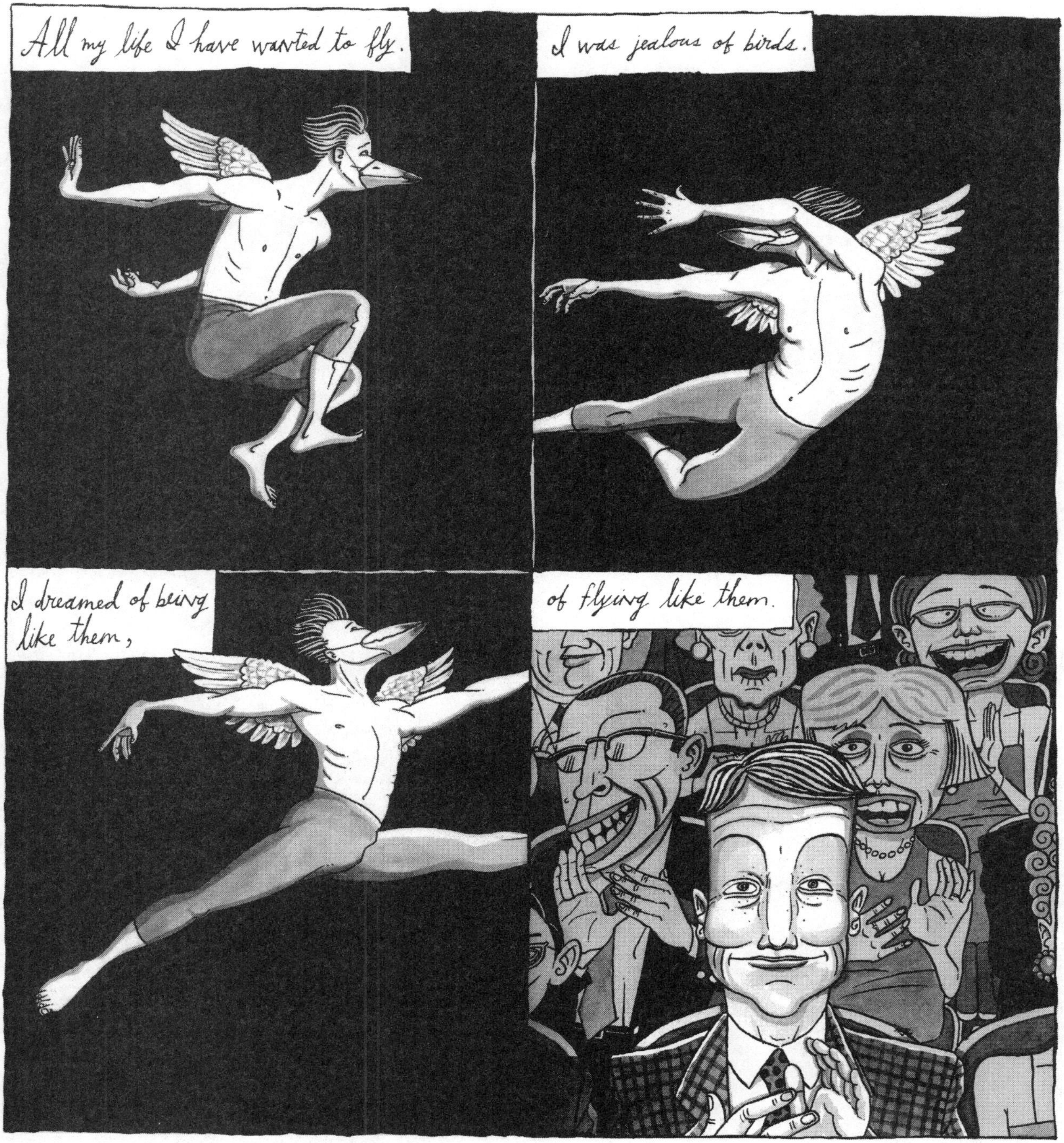
All my life I have wanted to fly.
I was jealous of birds.
I dreamed of being like them,
of flying like them.

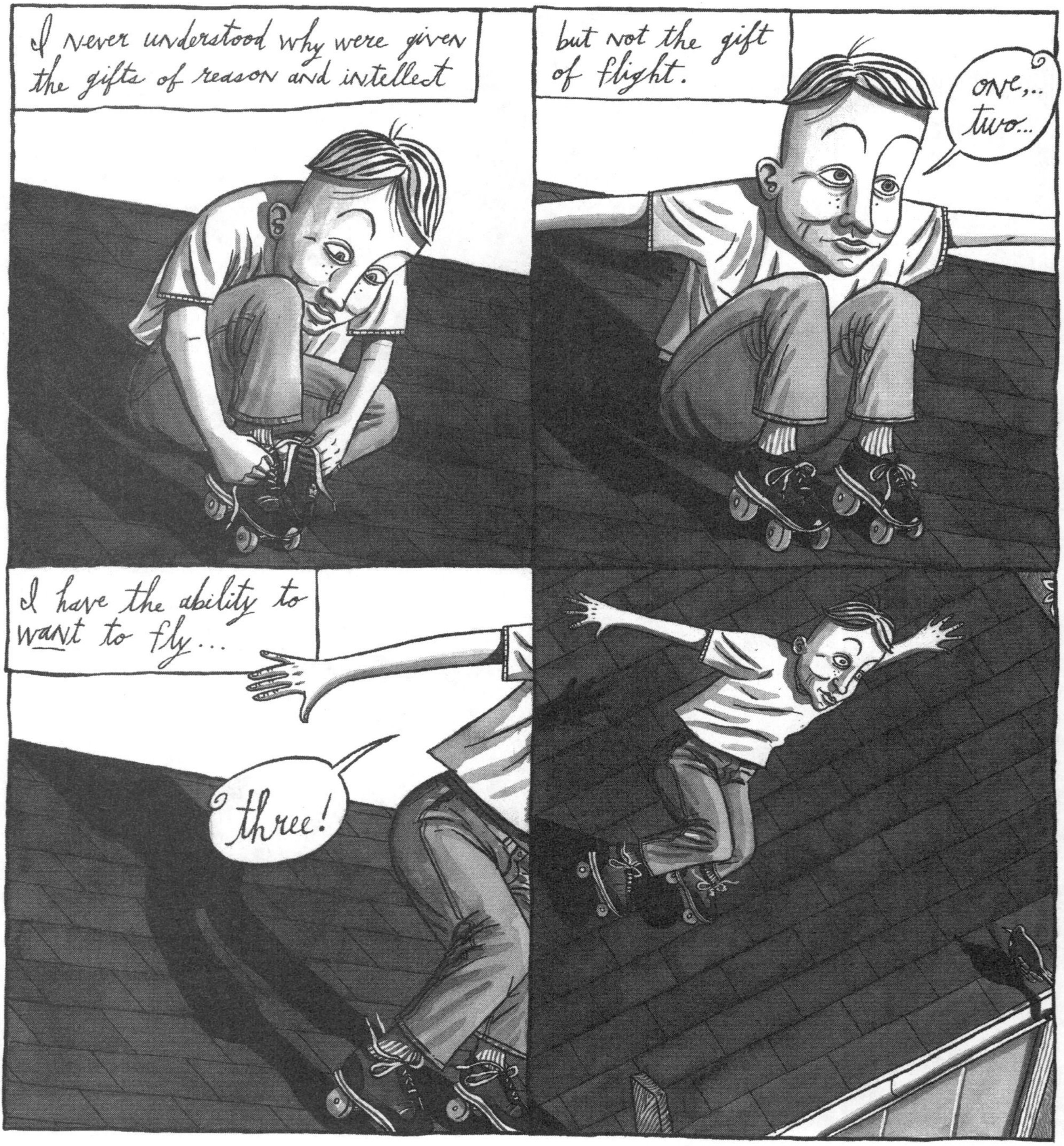
I never understood why we're given the gifts of reason and intellect
but not the gift of flight.
one,... two...
I have the ability to WANT to fly...
three!

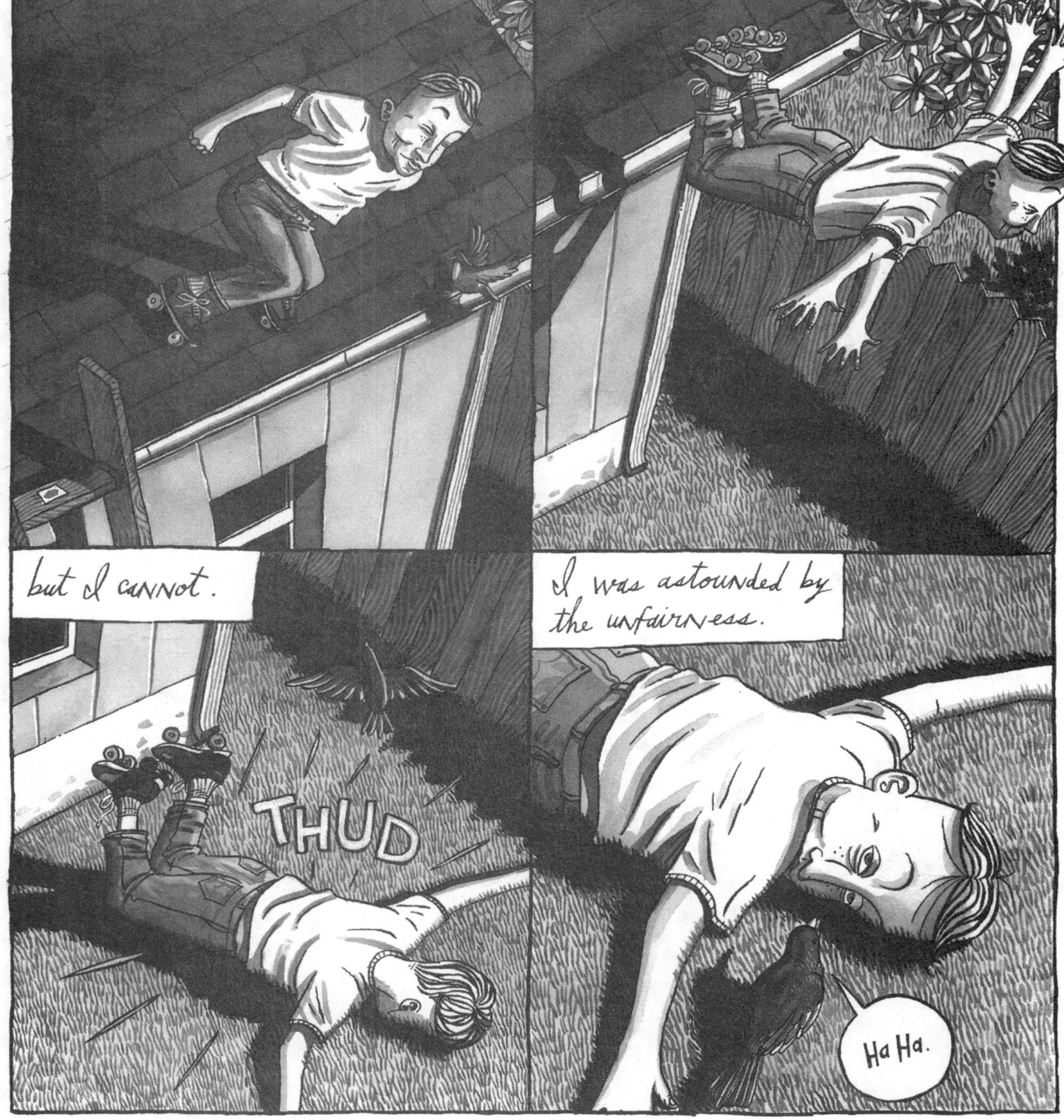

but I cannot.
THUD
I was astounded by the unfairness.
Ha Ha.

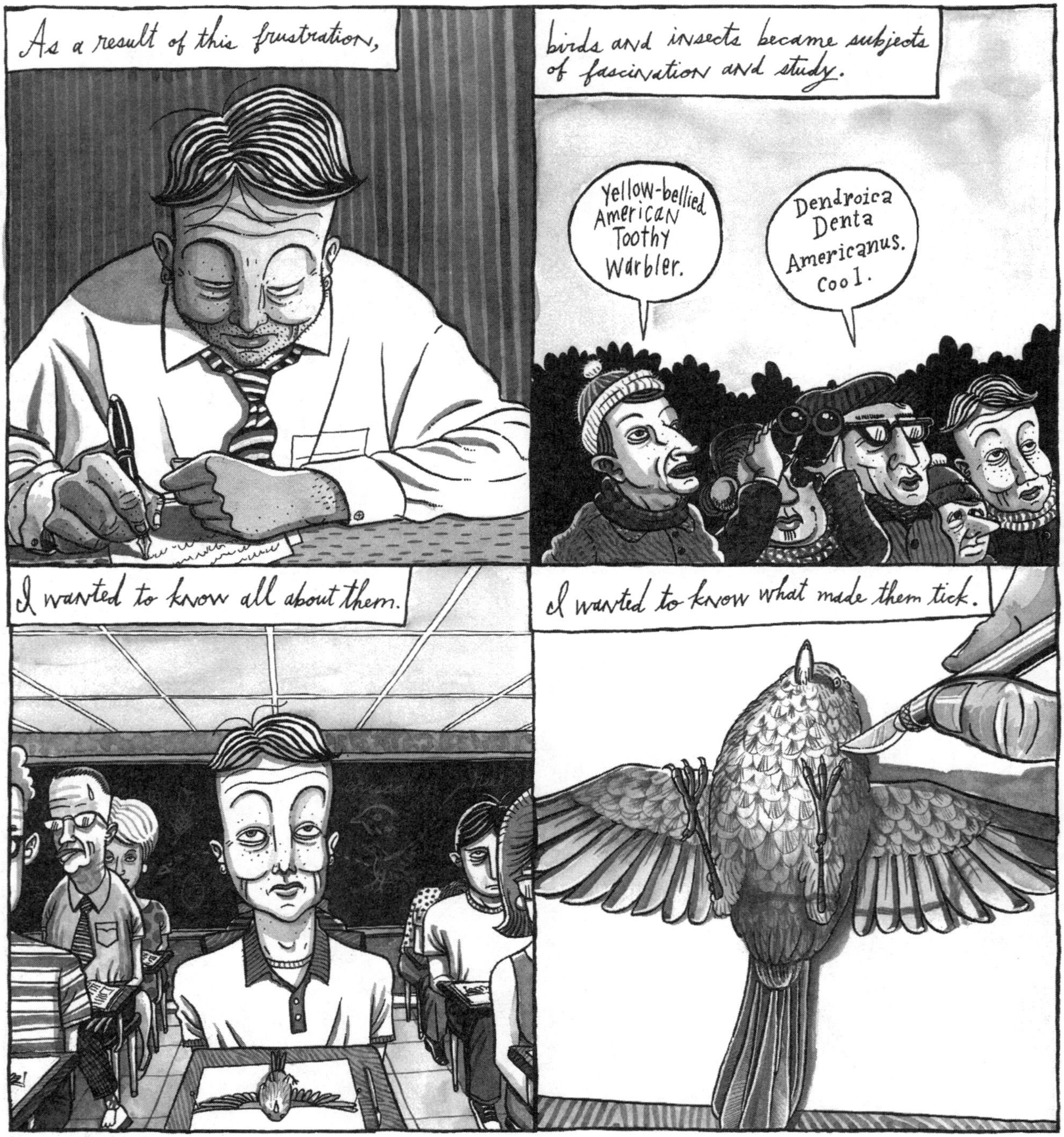
As a result of this frustration,
birds and insects became subjects of fascination and study.
Yellow-bellied American Toothy Warbler.
Dendroica Denta Americanus. Cool.
I wanted to know all about them.
I wanted to know what made them tick.

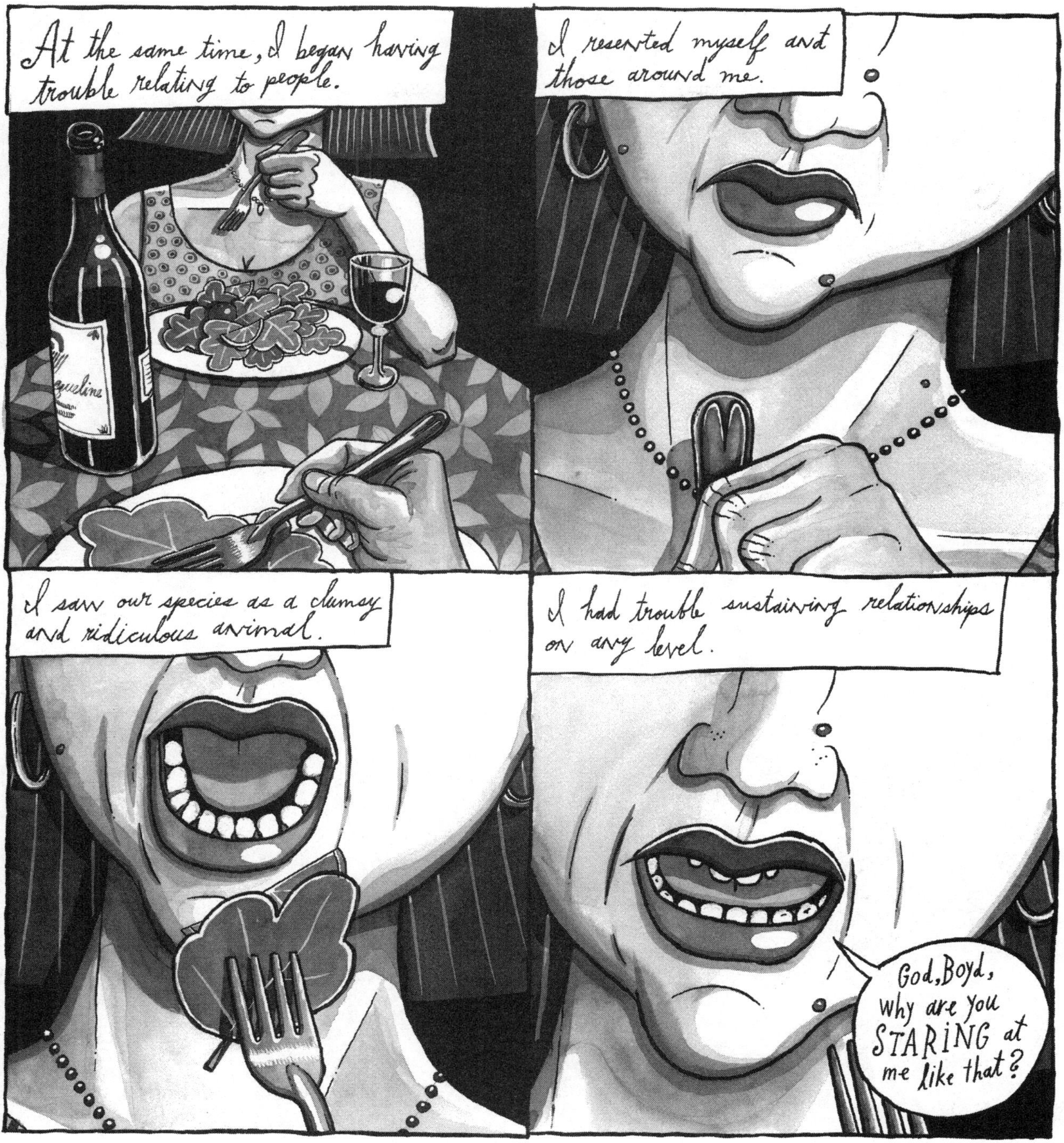
At the same time, I began having trouble relating to people.
I resented myself and those around me.
I saw our species as a clumsy and ridiculous animal.
I had trouble sustaining relationships on any level.
God, Boyd, why are you STARING at me like that?

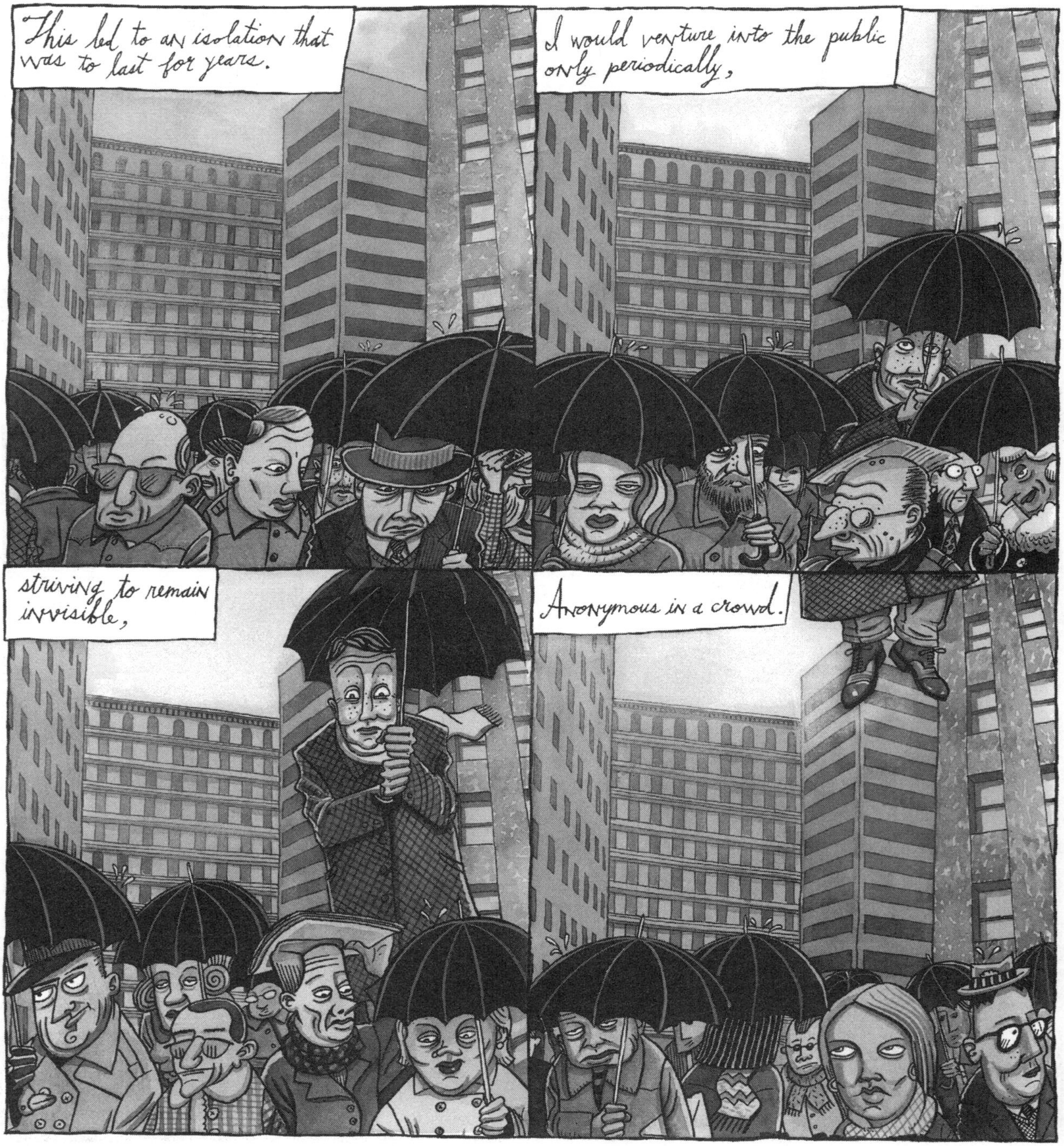
This led to an isolation that was to last for years.
I would venture into the public only periodically,
striving to remain invisible,
Anonymous in a crowd.

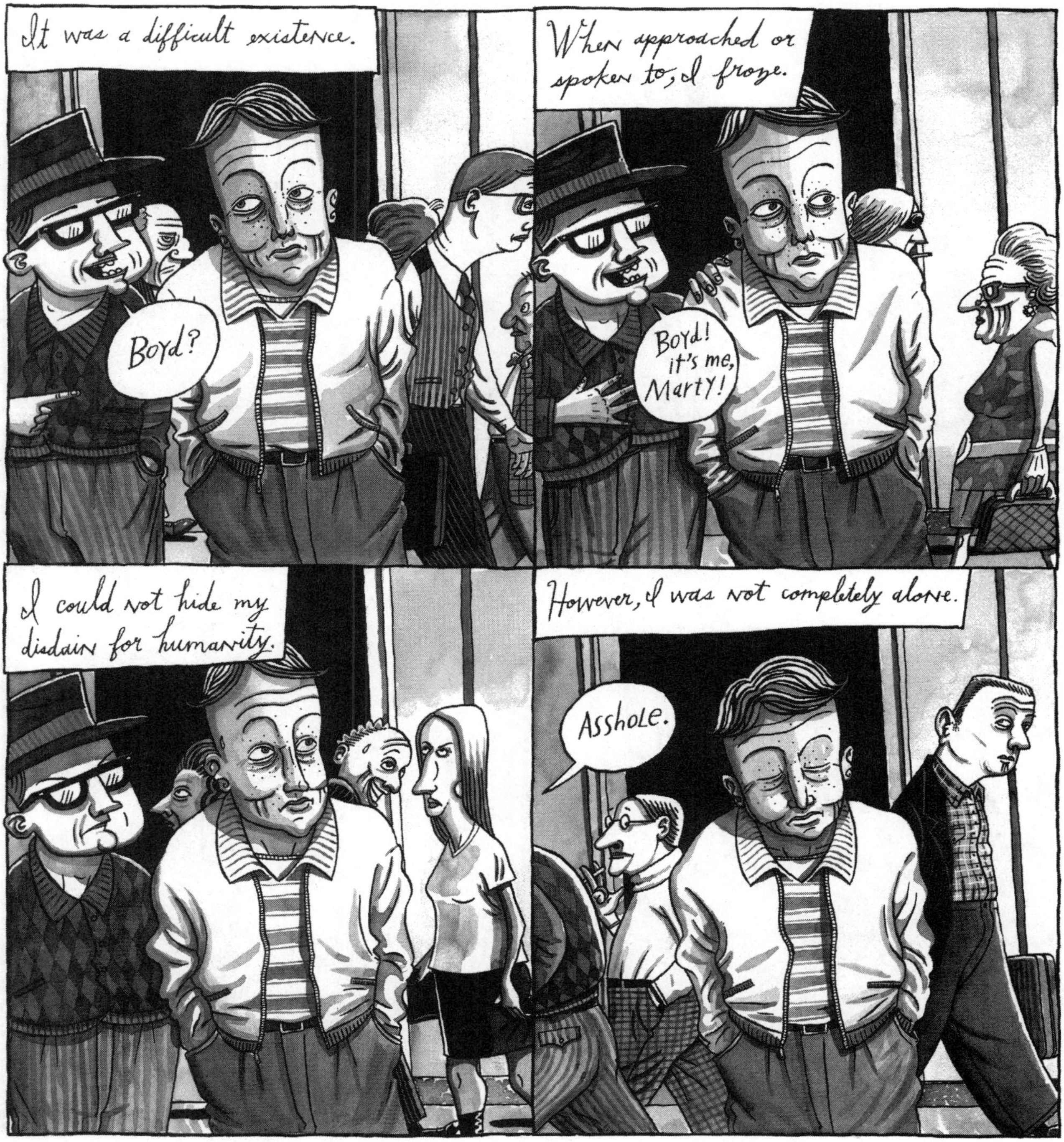
It was a difficult existence.
Boyd?
When approached or spoken to, I froze.
Boyd! it's me, Marty!
I could not hide my disdain for humanity.
However, I was not completely alone.
Asshole.

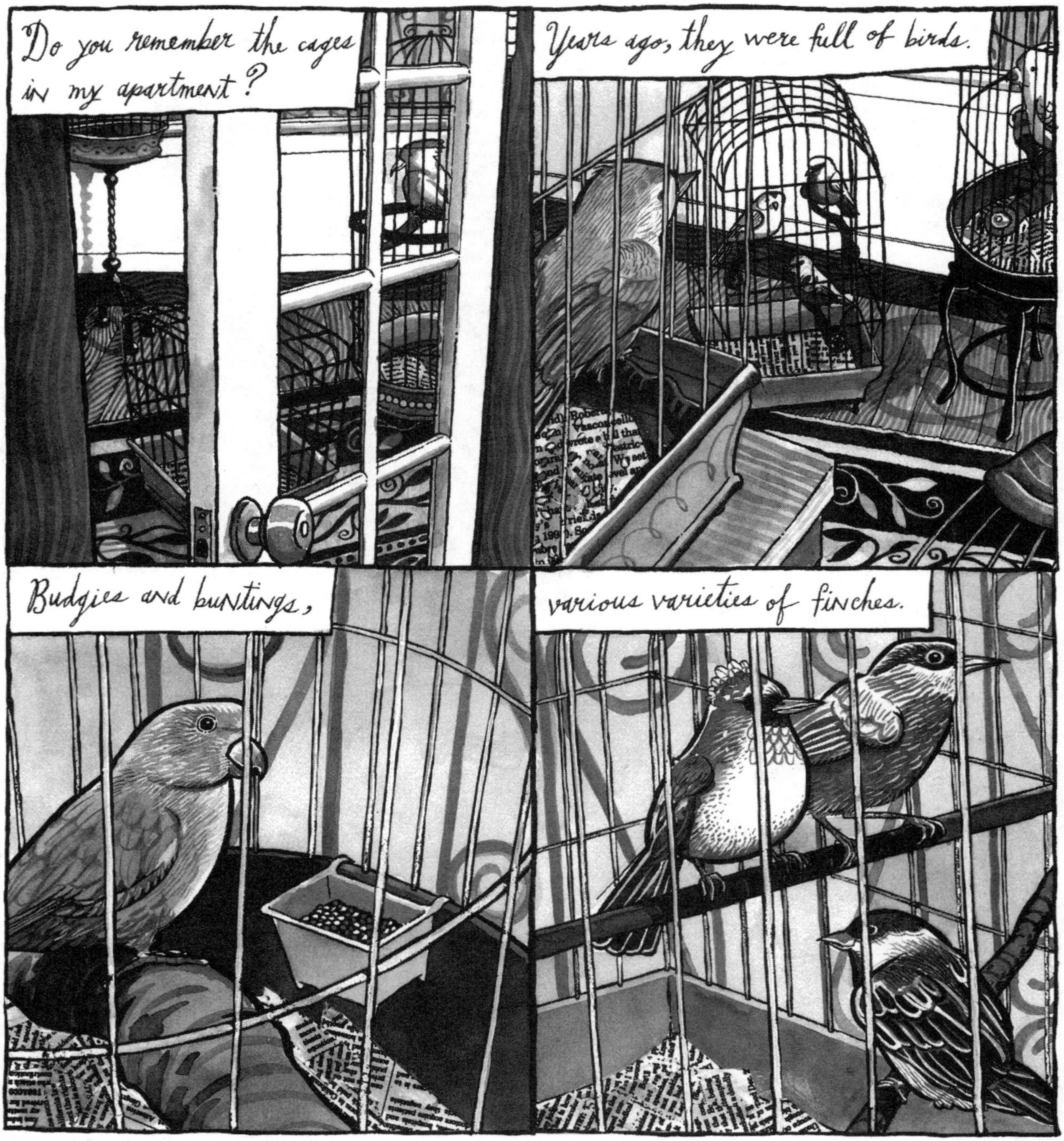
Do you remember the cages in my apartment?
Years ago, they were full of birds.
Budgies and buntings,
various varieties of finches.

I had collections of butterflies, beetles,
mosquitoes, moths...
These were objects of my fascination
as well as envy.

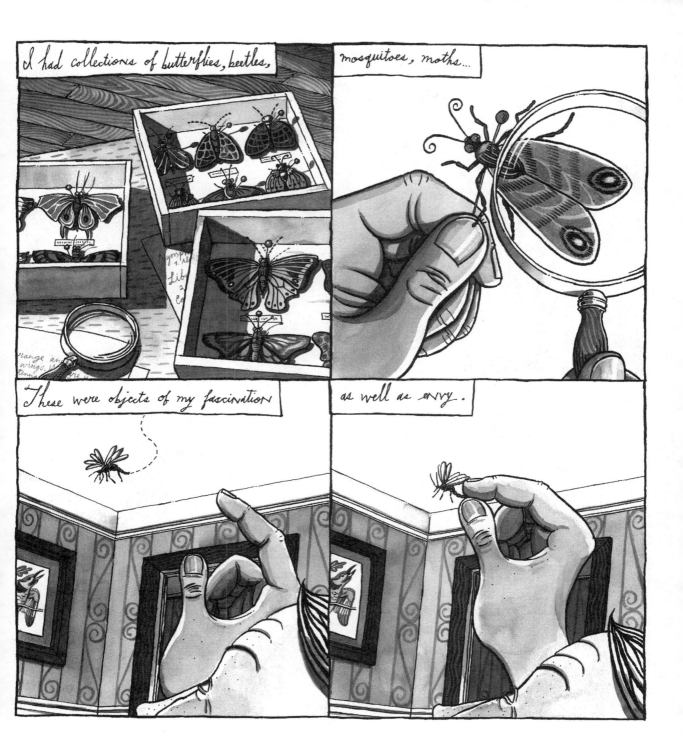

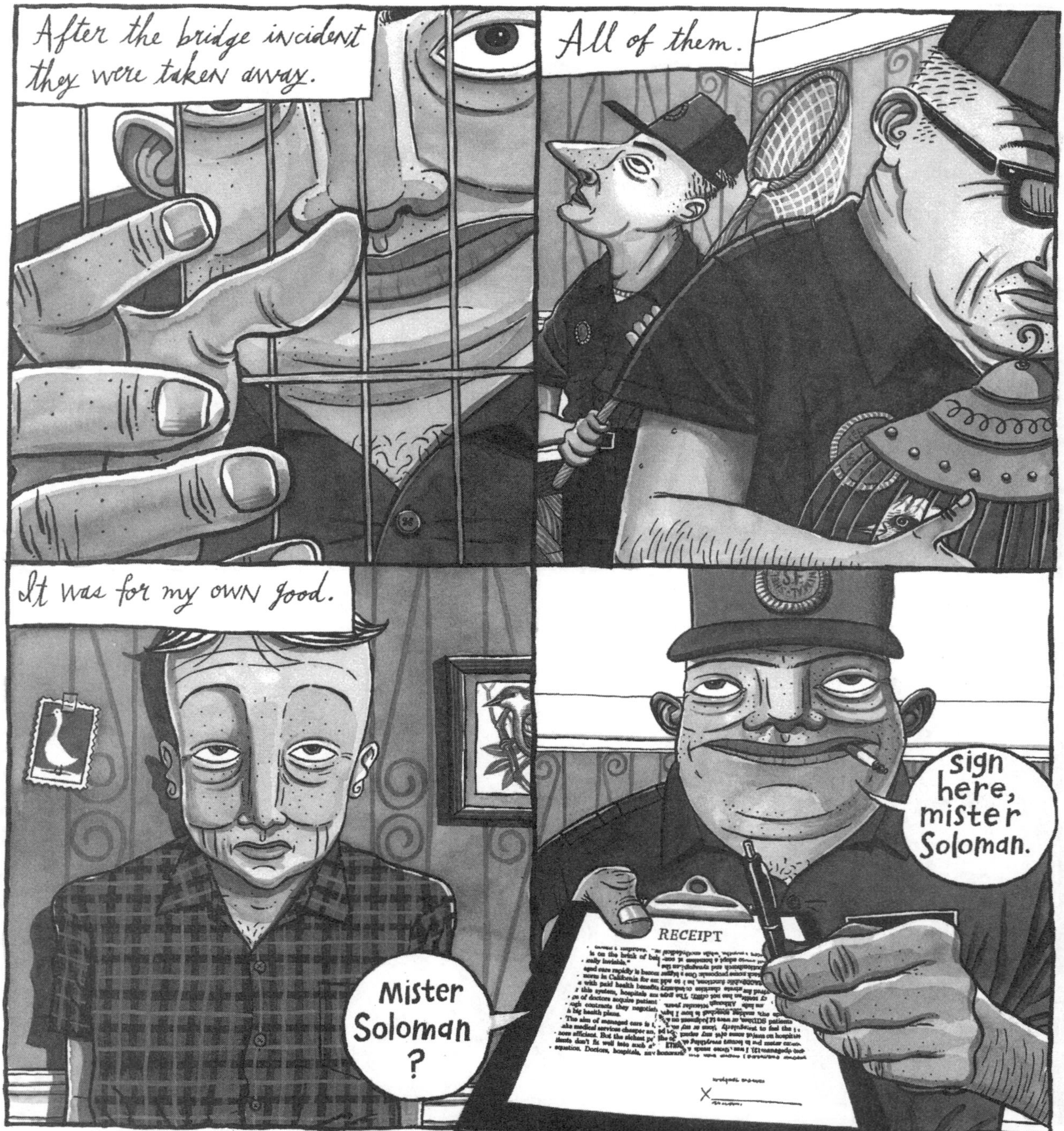
After the bridge incident they were taken away.
All of them.
It was for my OWN good.
Mister Soloman ?
sign here, mister Soloman.
RECEIPT

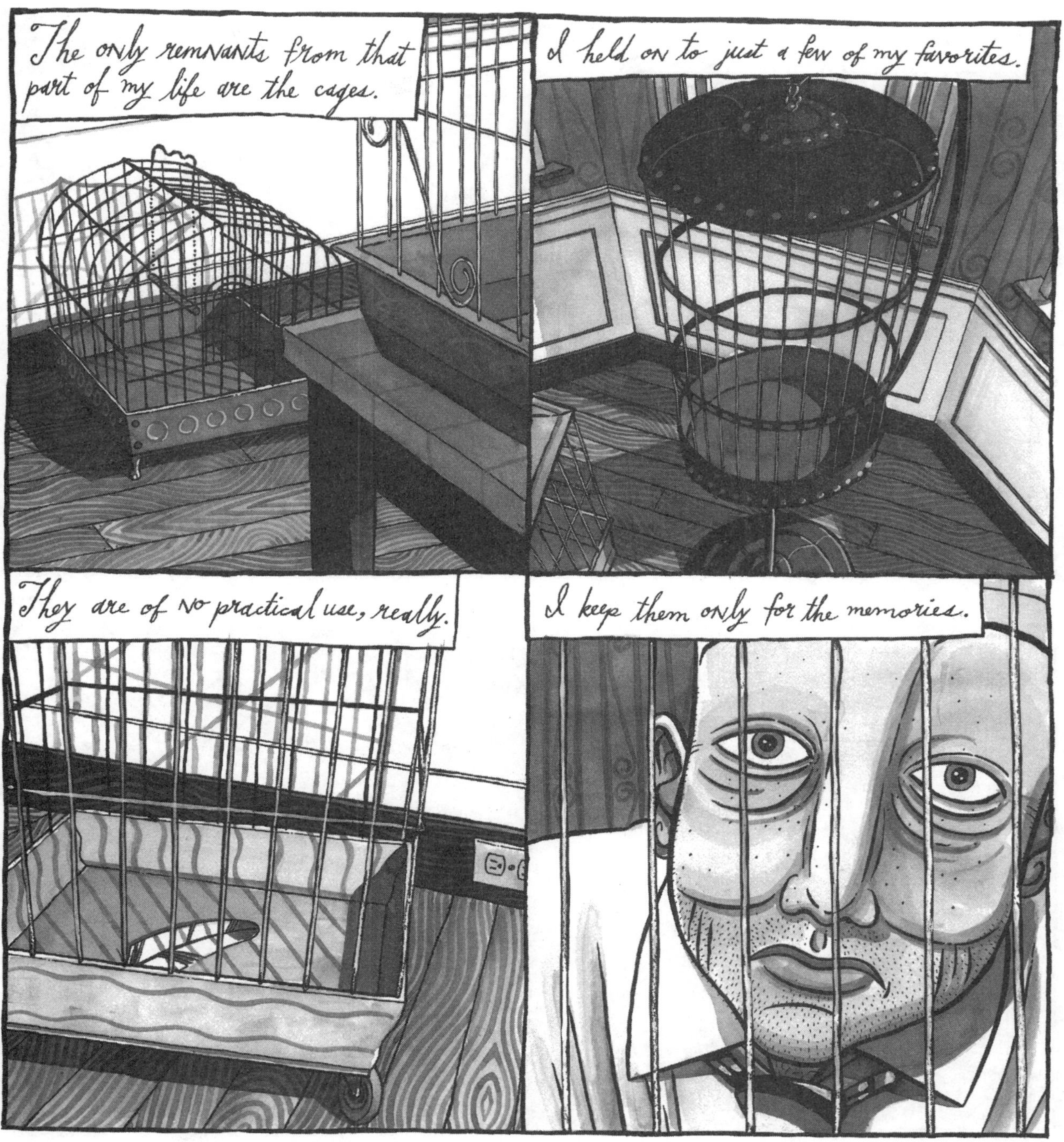

The only remnants from that part of my life are the cages.
I held on to just a few of my favorites.
They are of no practical use, really.
I keep them only for the memories.

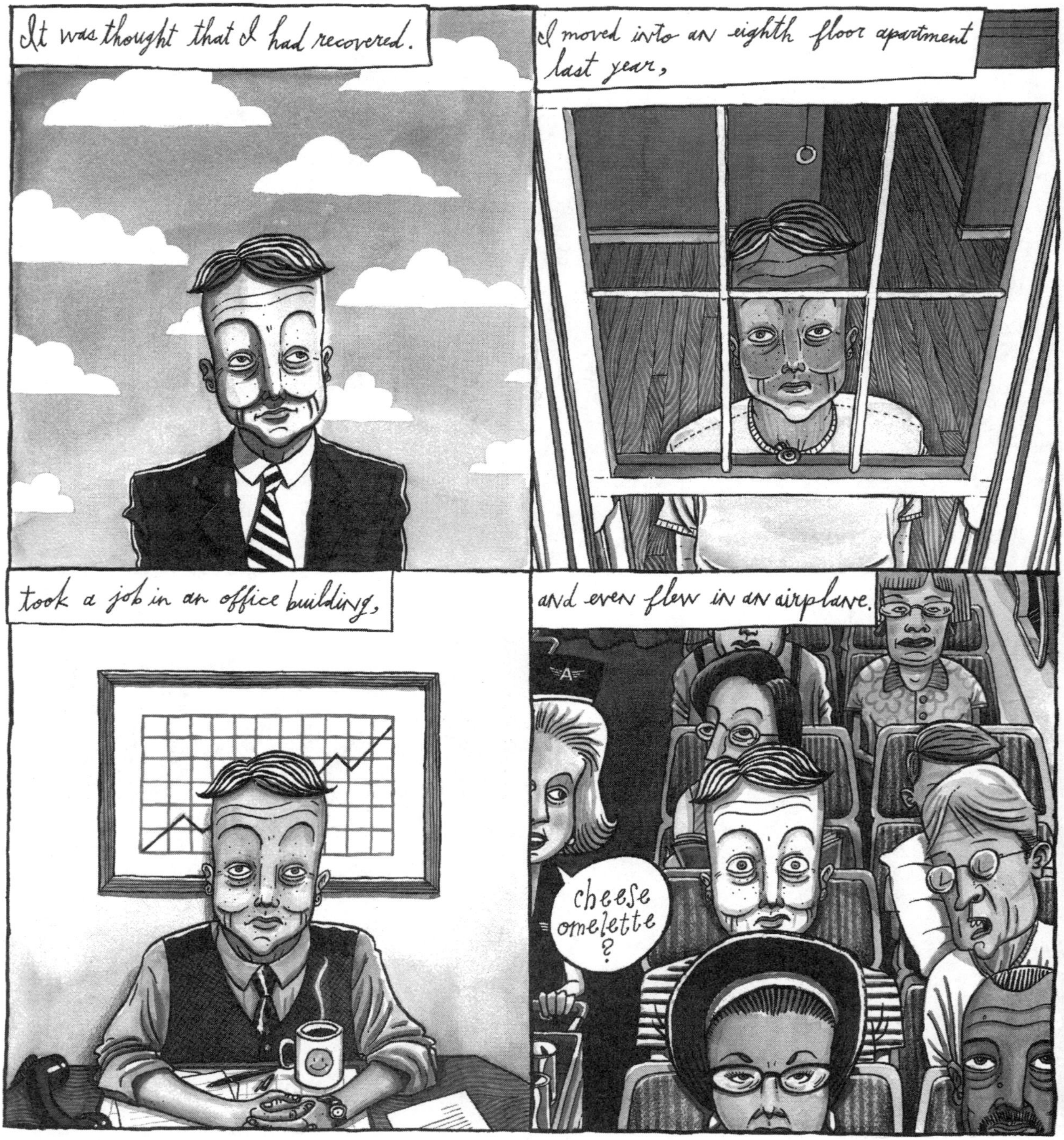
It was thought that I had recovered.
I moved into an eighth floor apartment last year,
took a job in an office building,
and even flew in an airplane.
cheese omelette ?

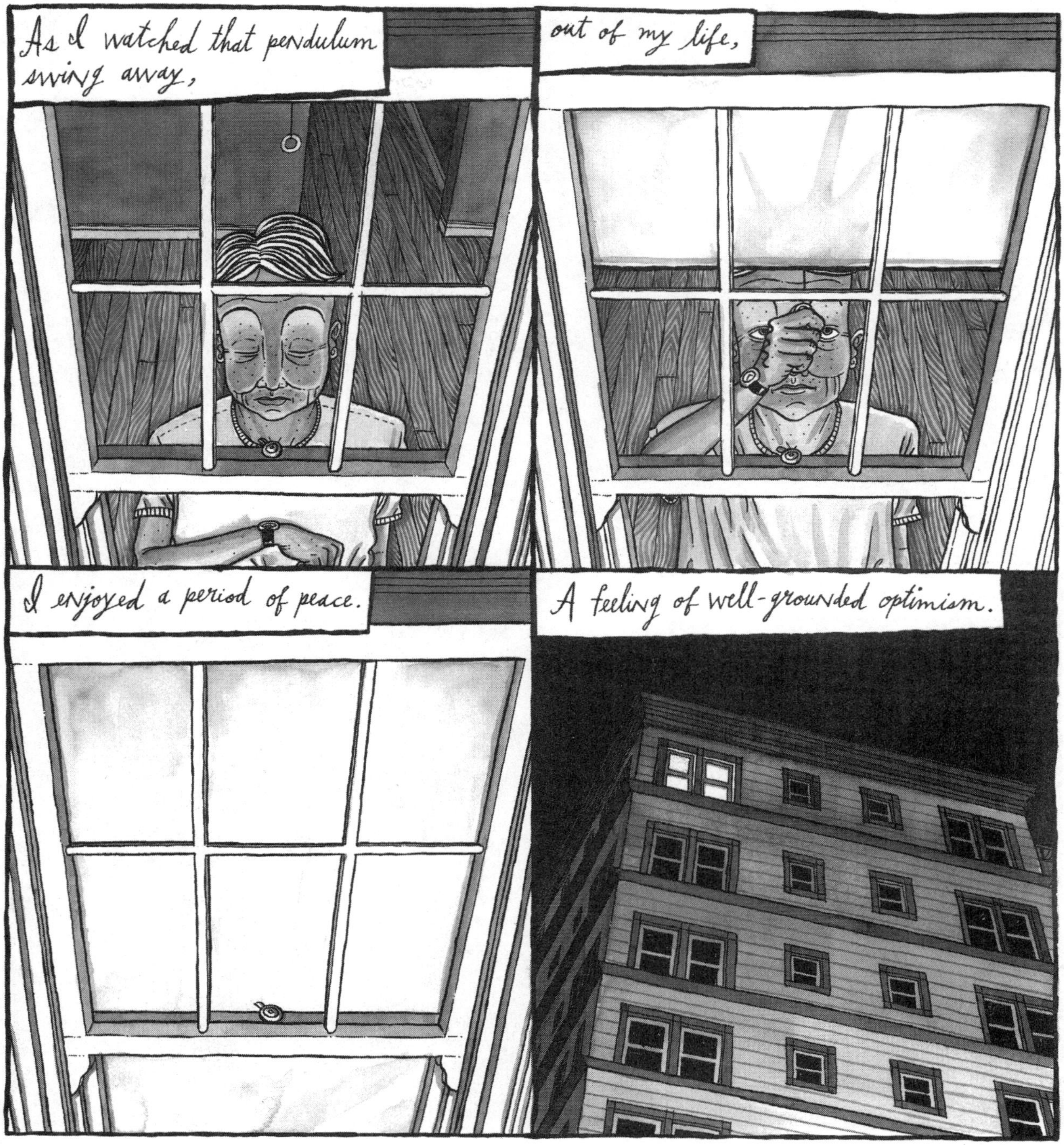
As I watched that pendulum swing away,
out of my life,
I enjoyed a period of peace.
A feeling of well-grounded optimism.

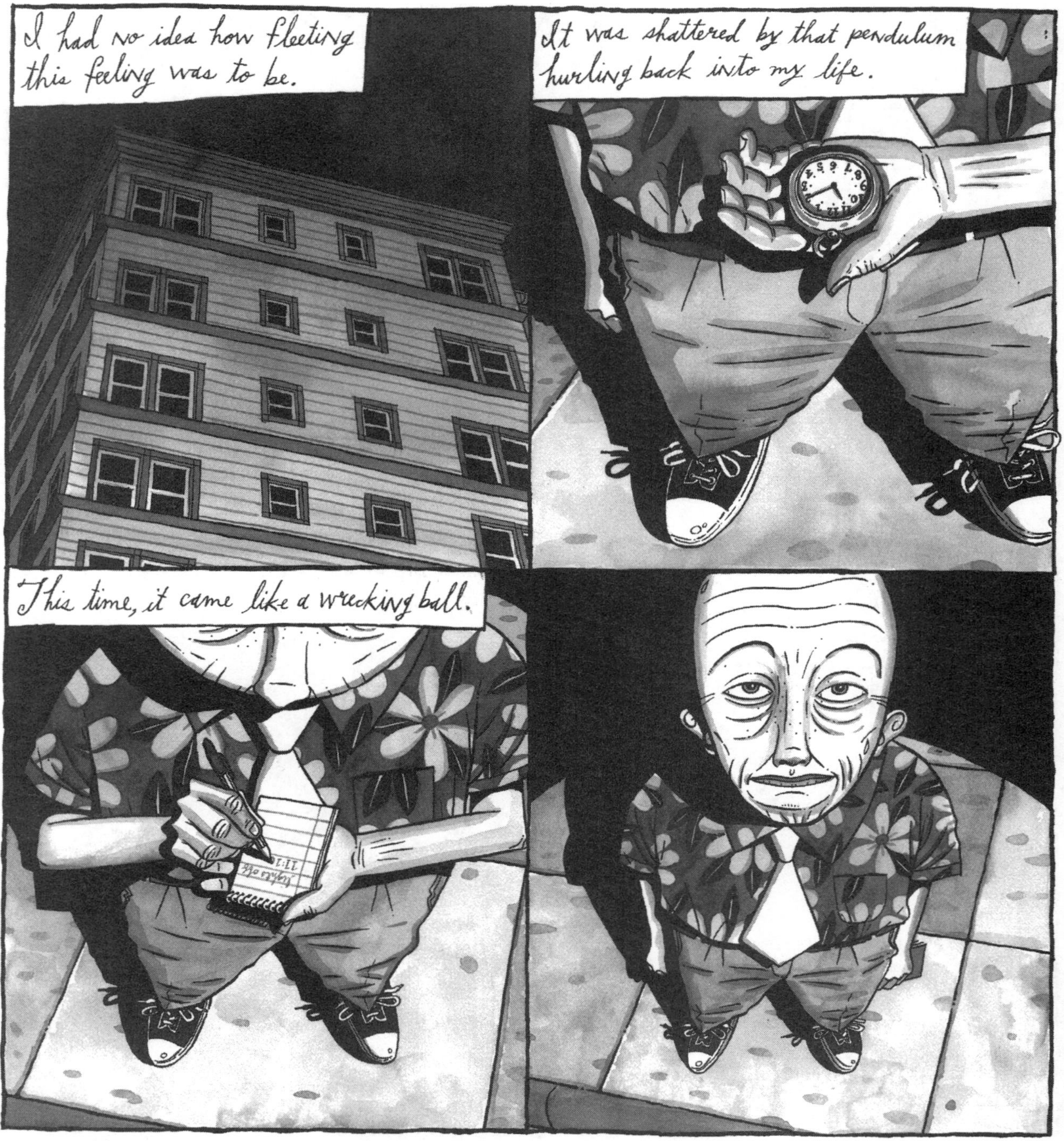
I had no idea how fleeting this feeling was to be.
It was shattered by that pendulum hurling back into my life.
This time, it came like a wrecking ball.

THree

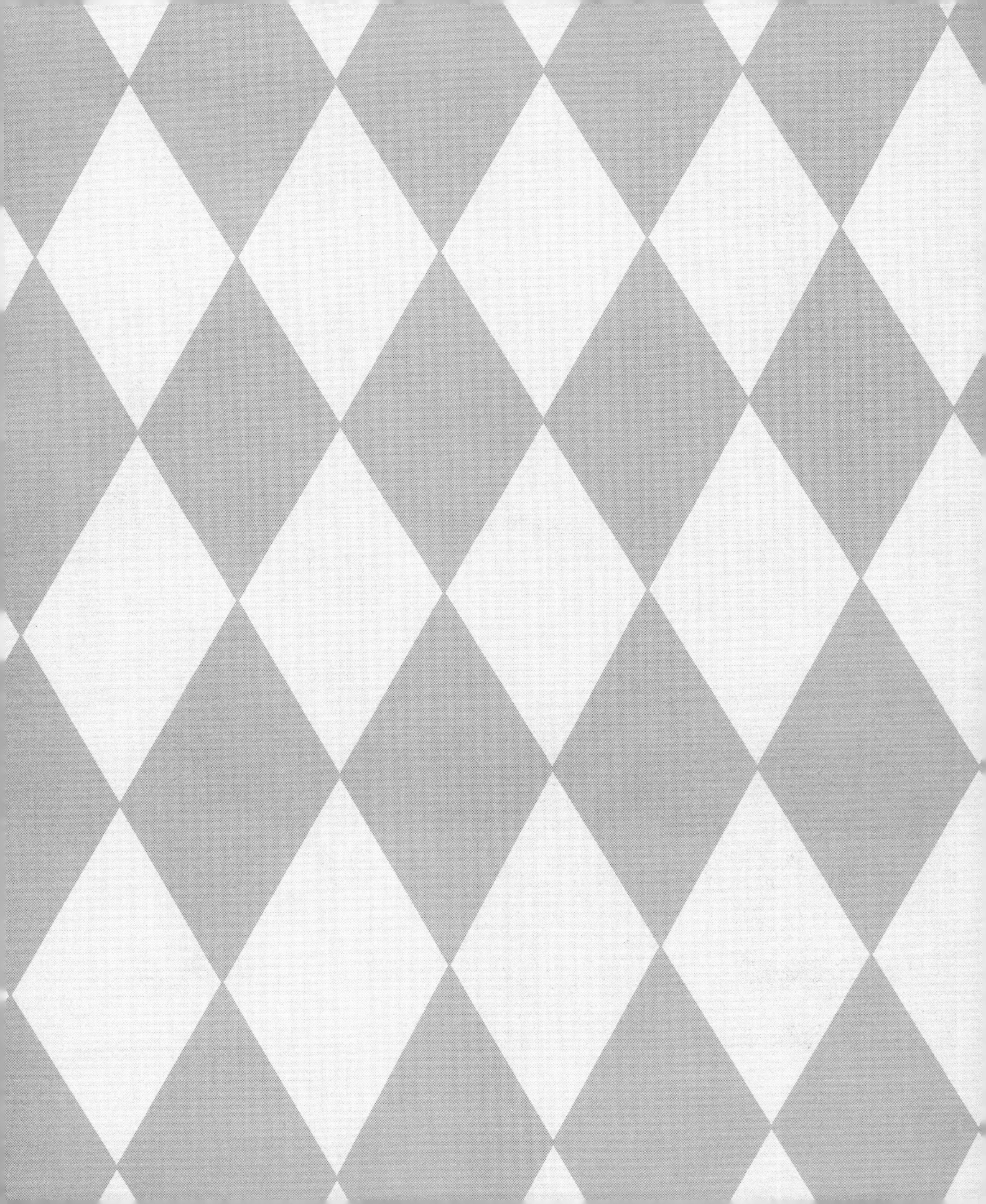

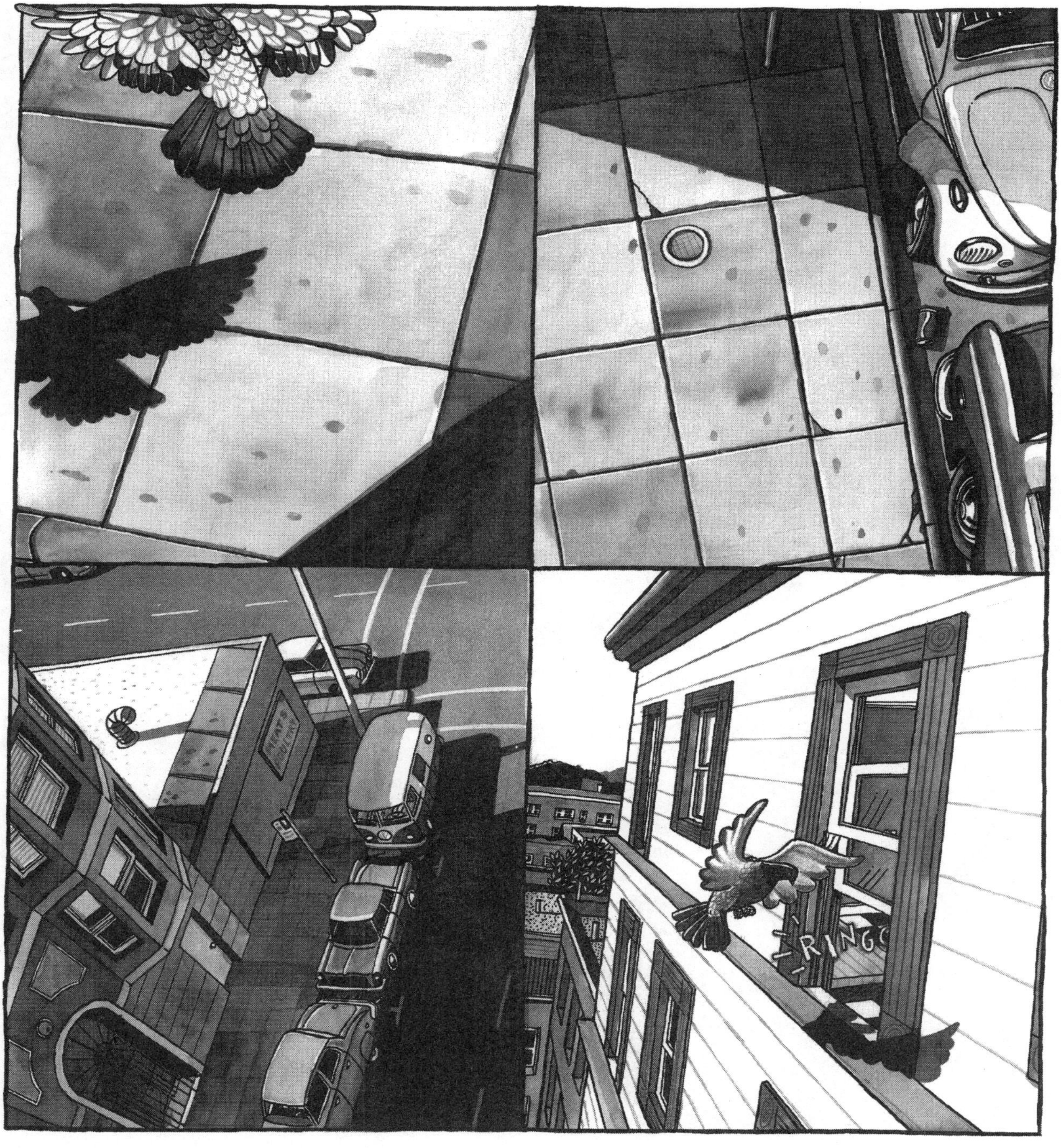
RING

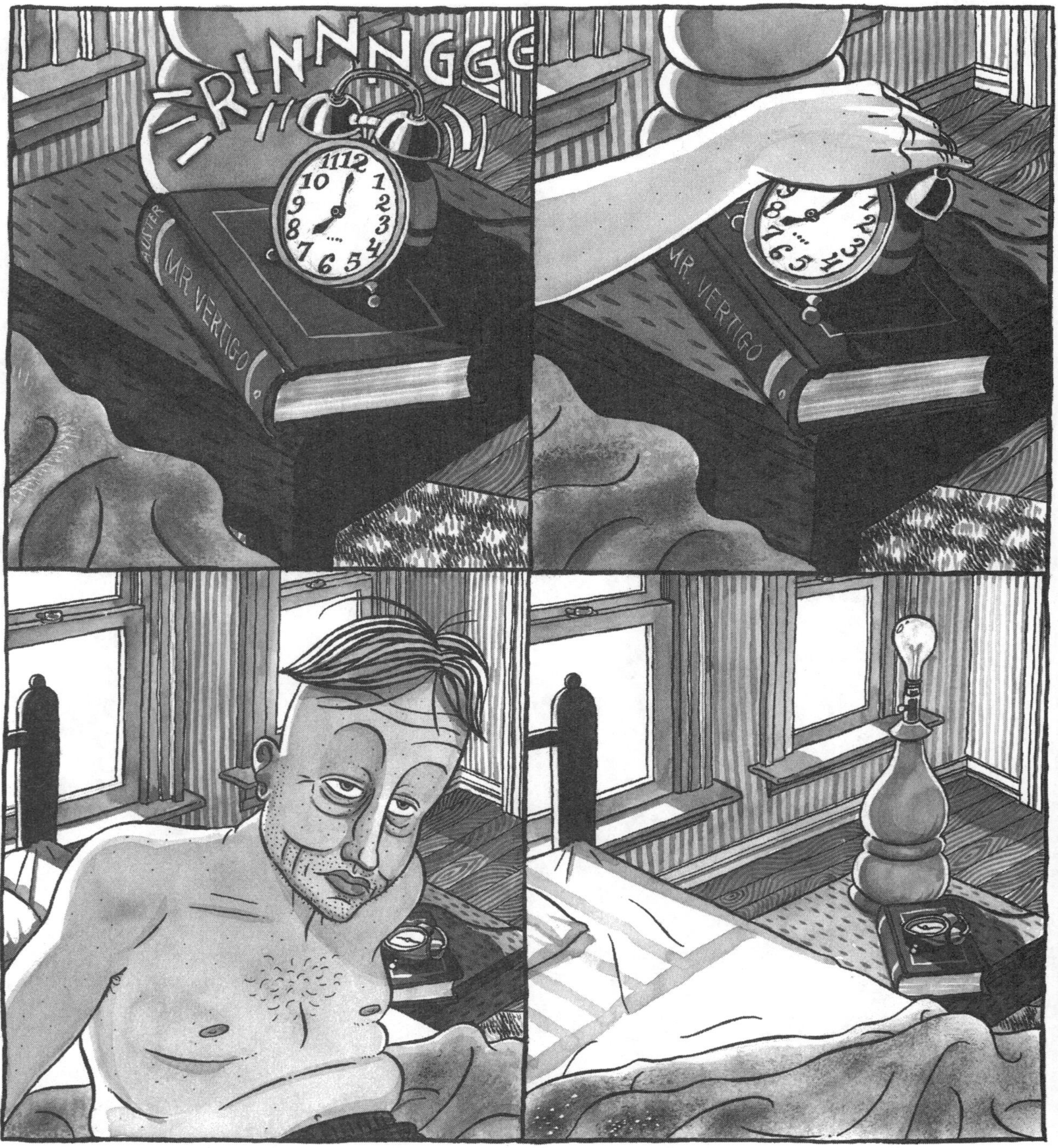
RINNNGGG
AUSTER
MR VERTIGO
MR. VERTIGO

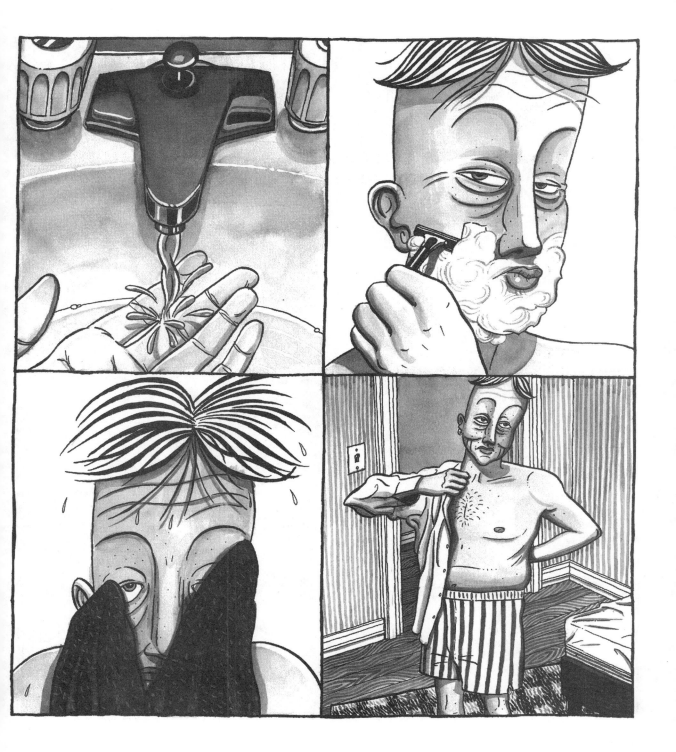

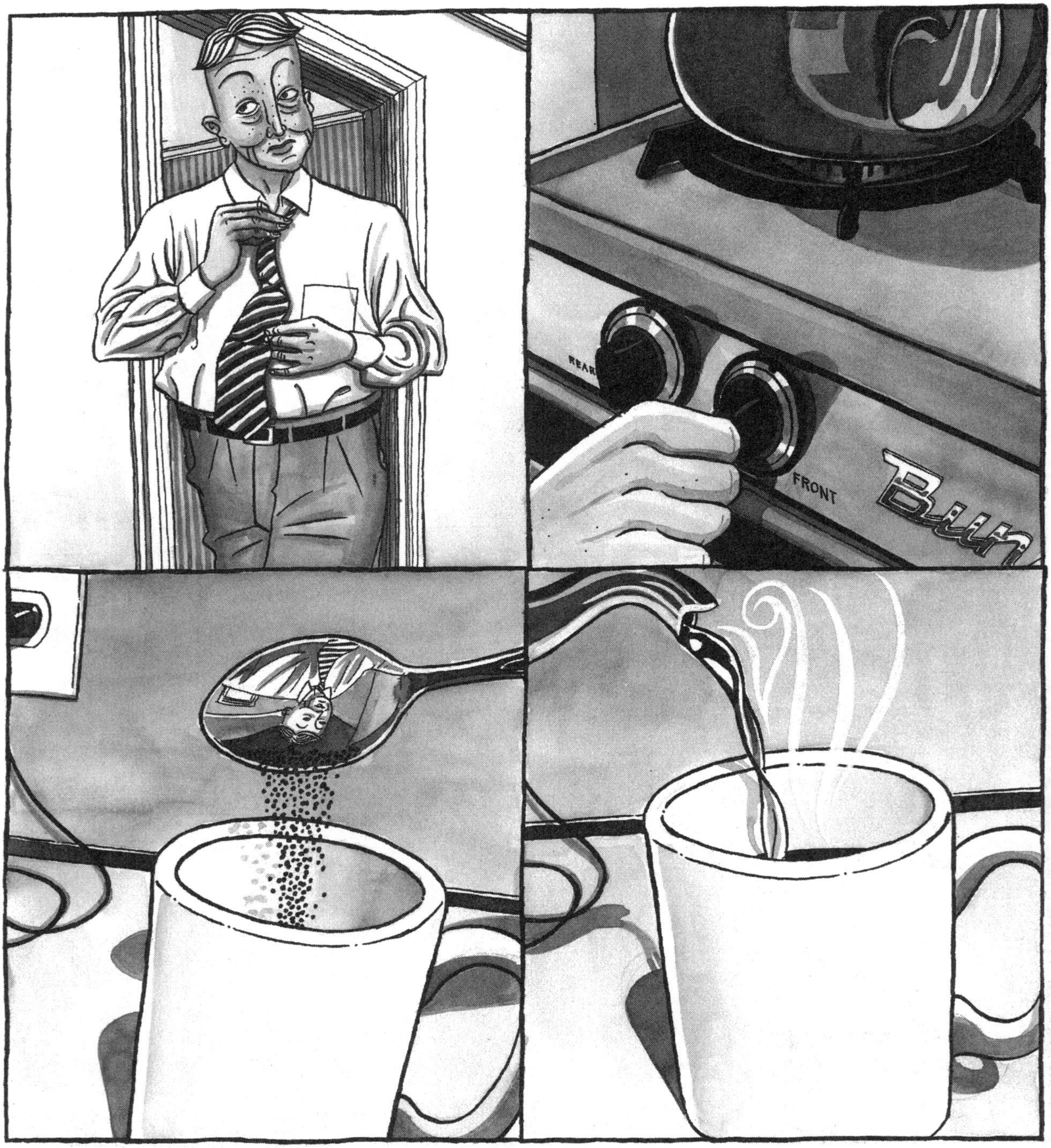
REAR
FRONT

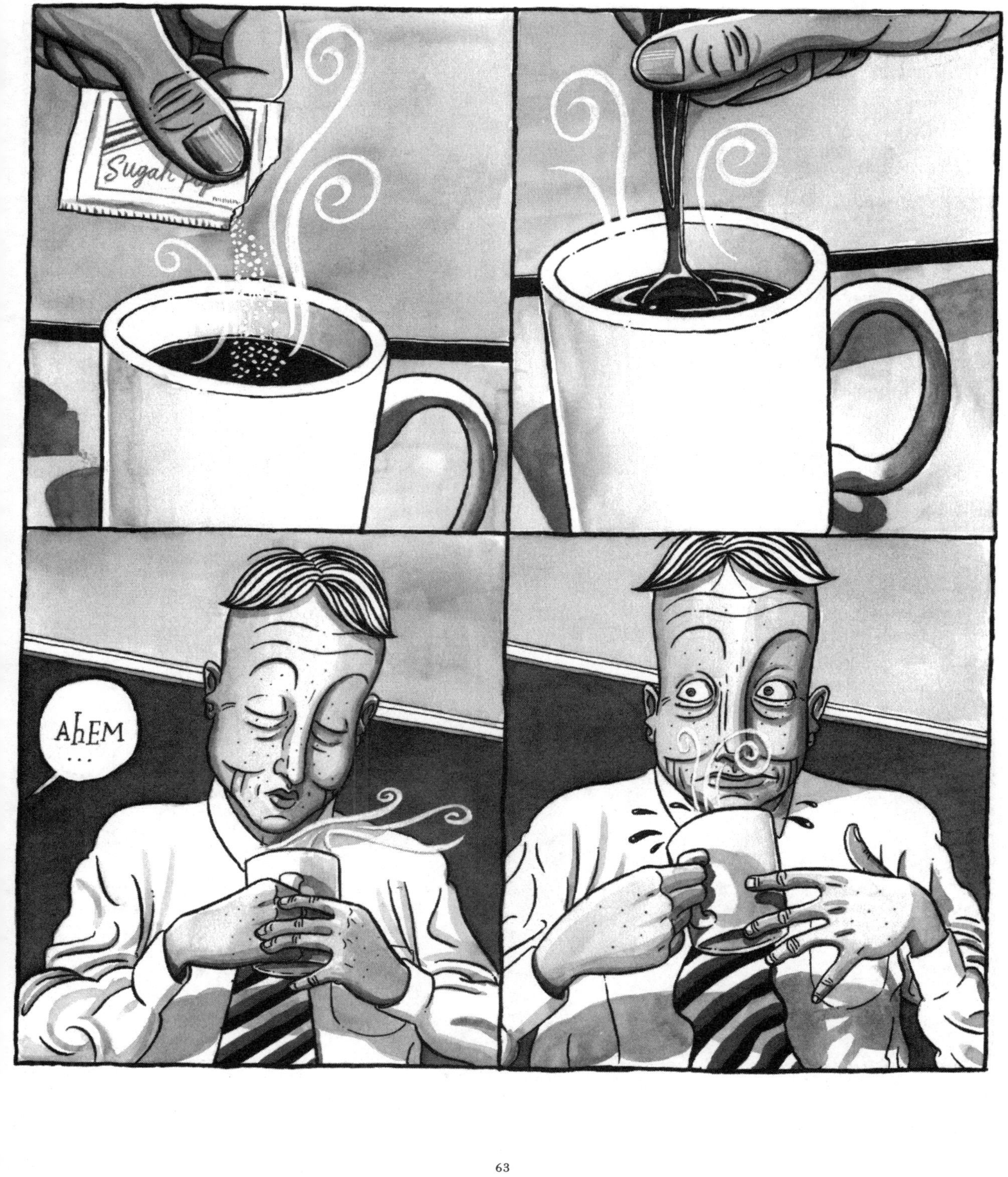
Sugah
AhEM ...

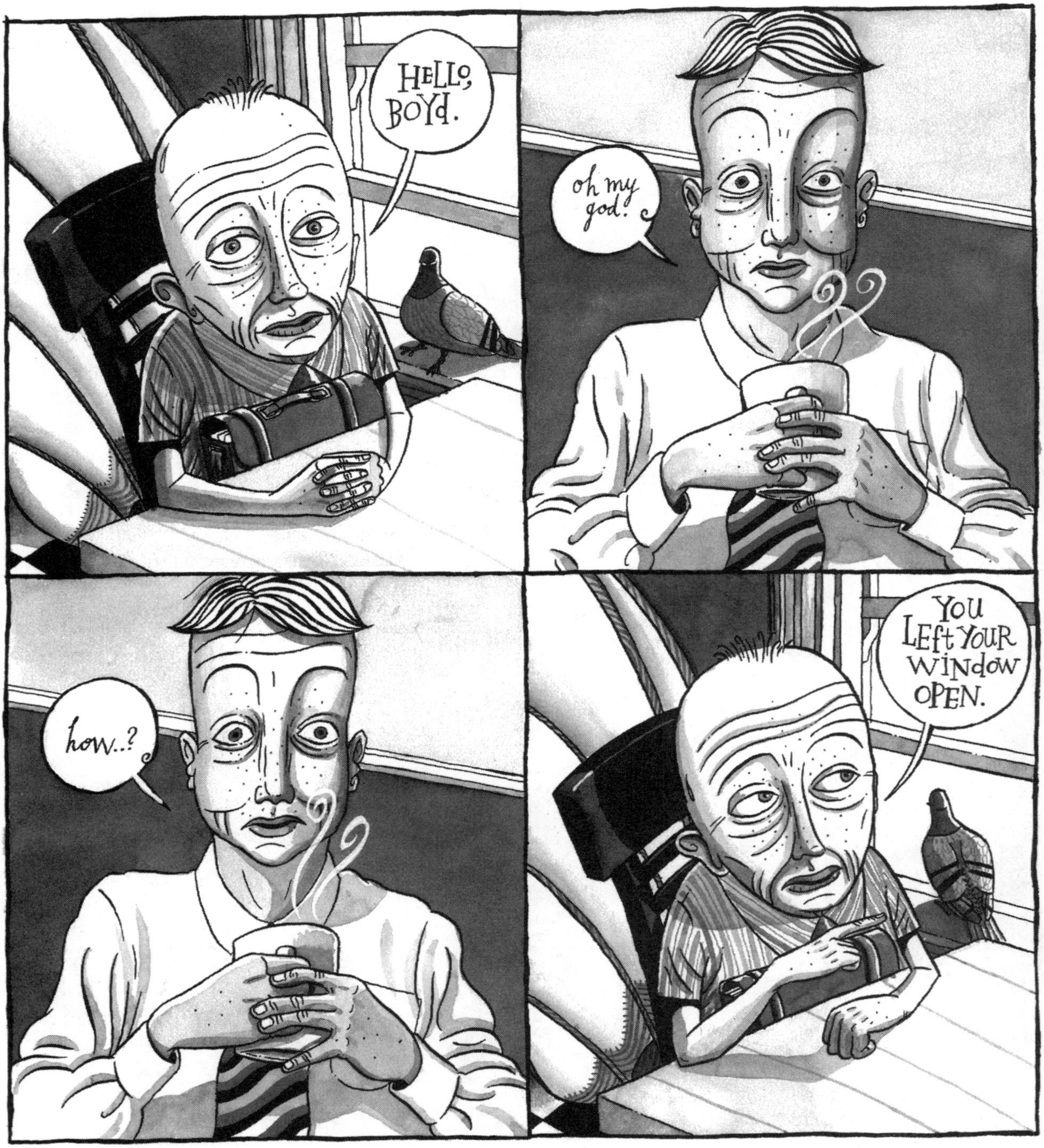
HELLO, BOYd.
oh my god.
how..?
YOU LEFT YOUR WINDOW OPEN.

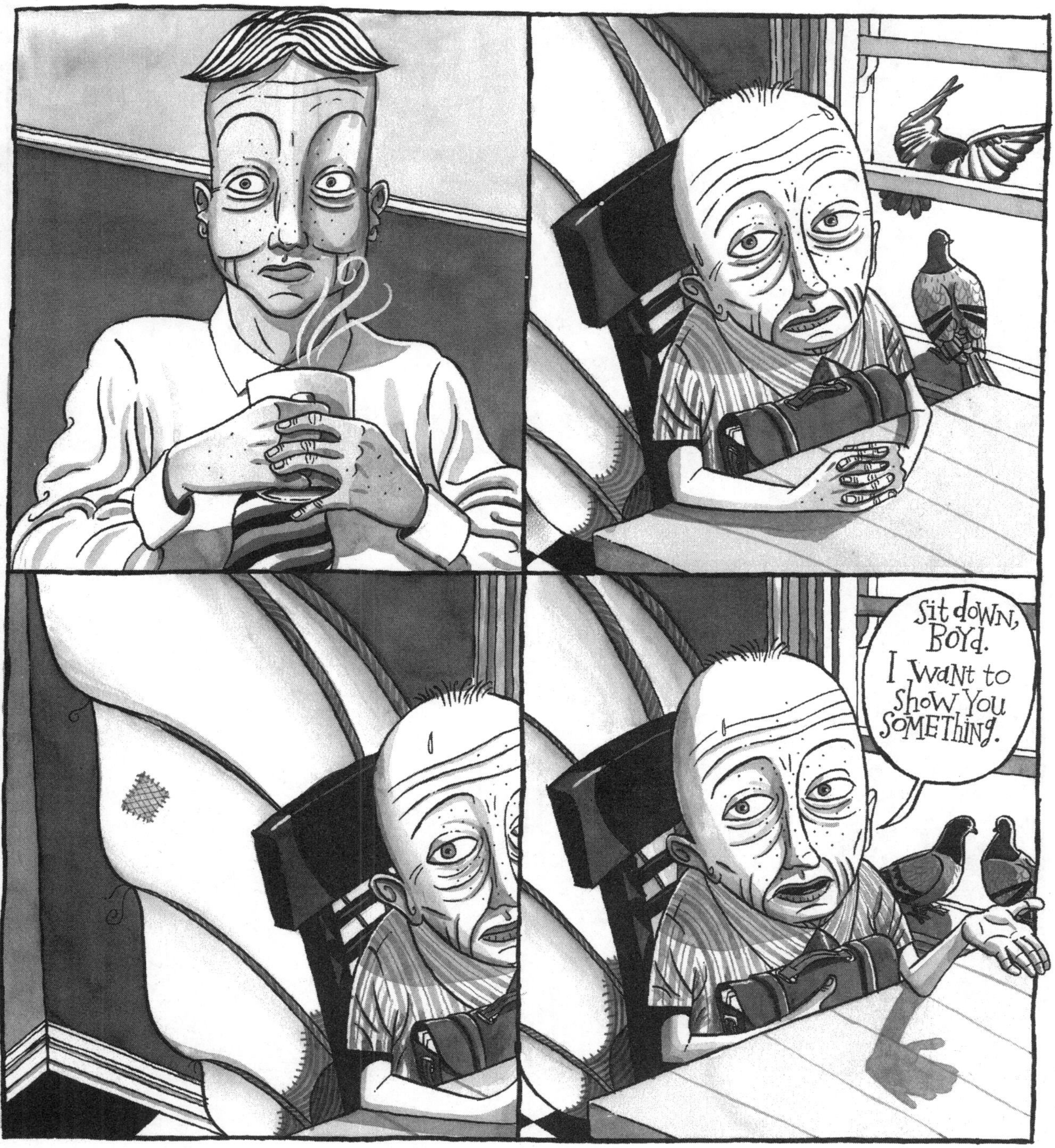
Sit down, Boyd. I want to show you something.

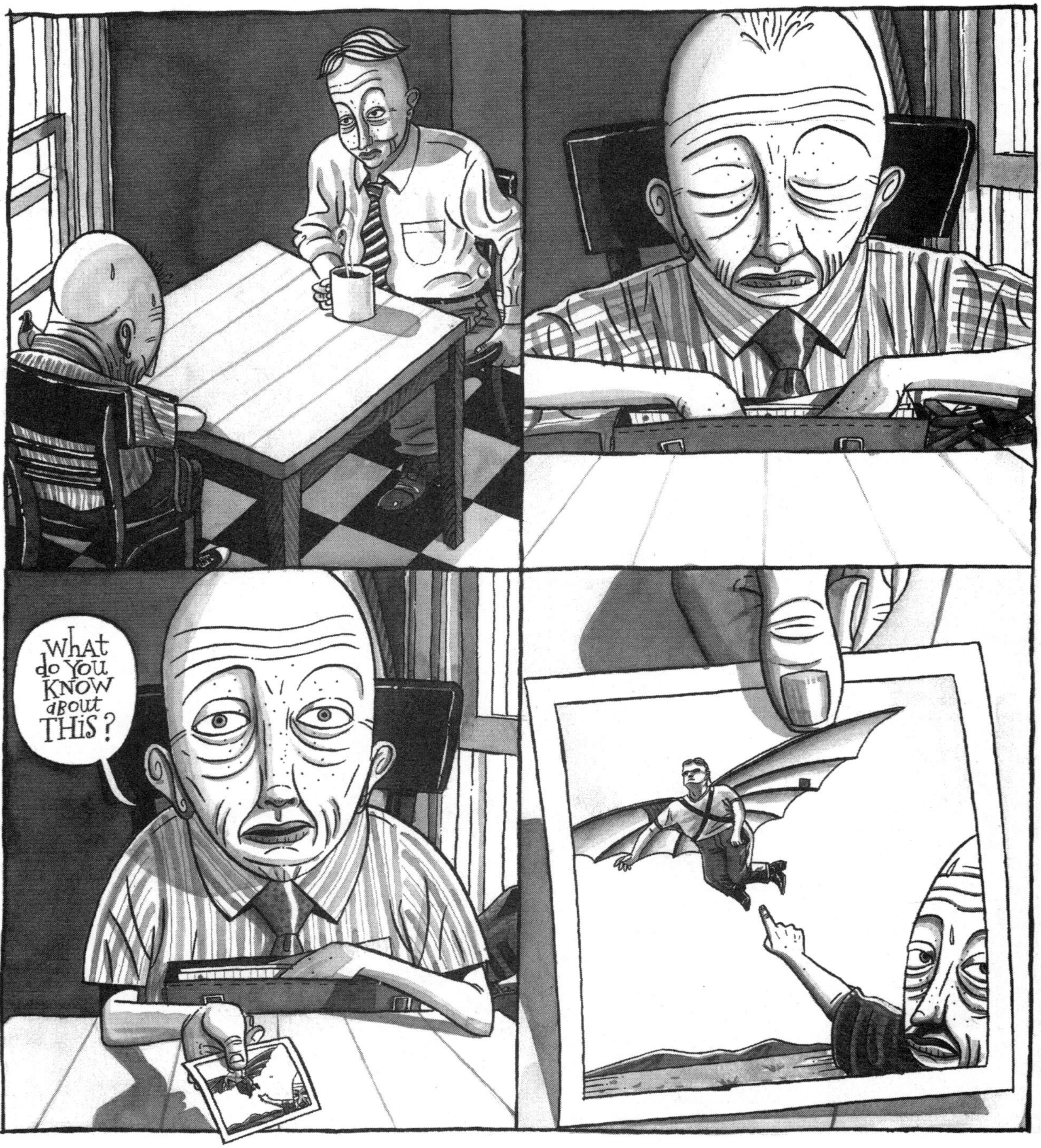
WHAt do YOU KNOW about THIS?

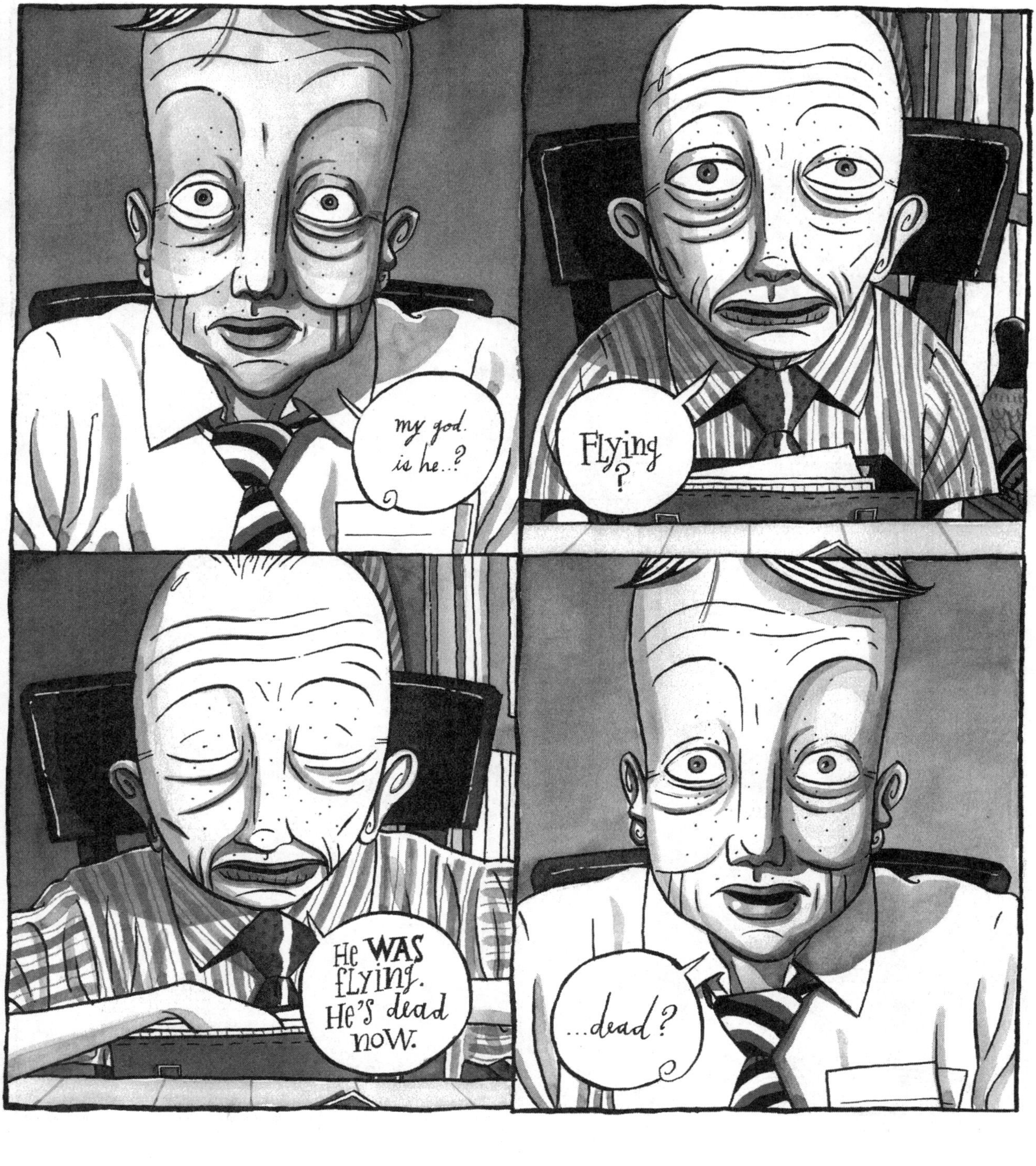
my god. is he..?
Flying ?
He WAS flying. He's dead now.
...dead?

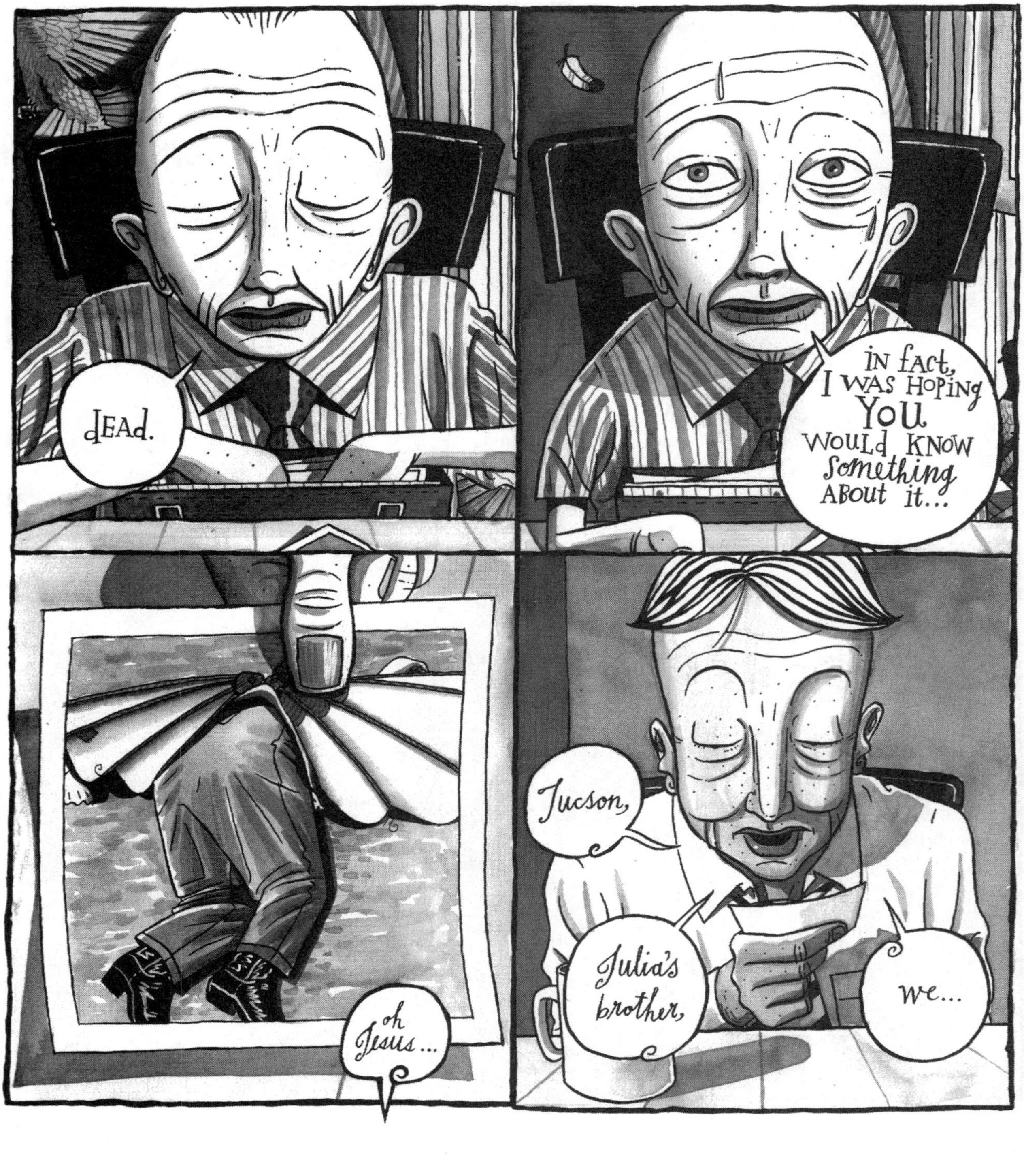
dEAd.
IN fact, I WAS HOPING YOU WOULd KNOW Something ABOUT it...
oh Jesus...
Tucson,
Julia's brother,
we...

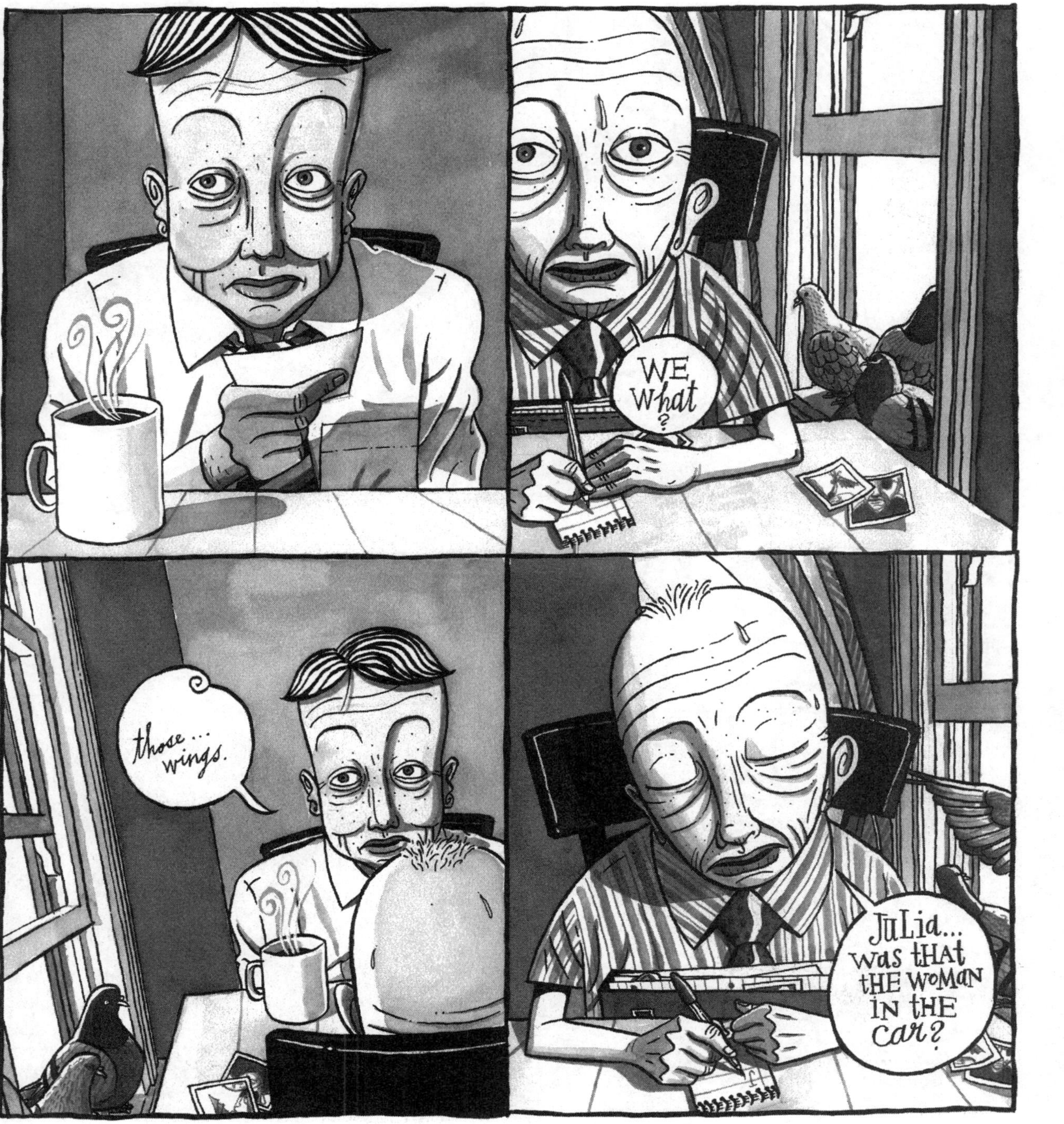
WE what?
those... wings.
JuLia... was tHAt tHE WoMan in tHE car?

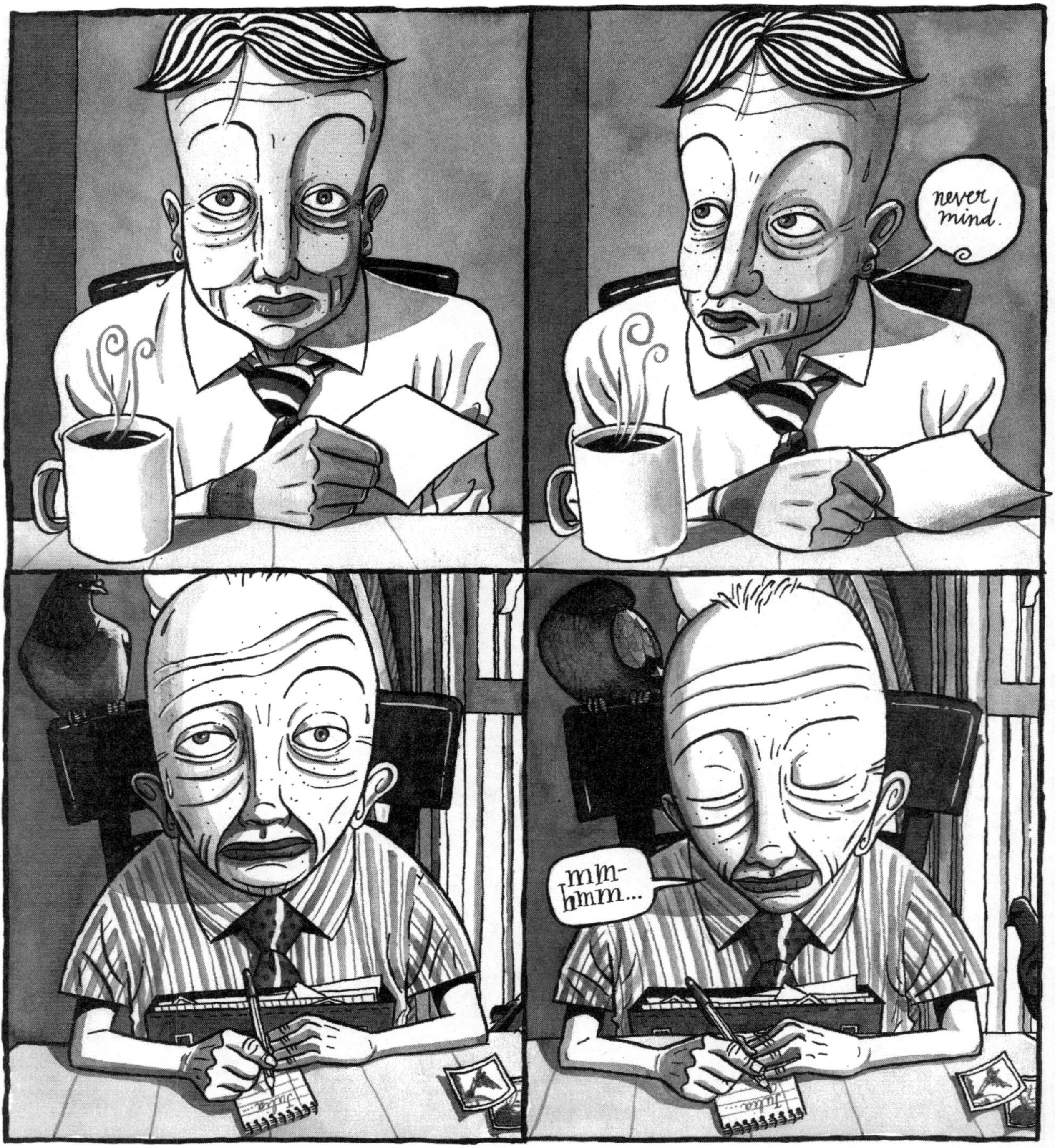
never mind.
mm-hmm...

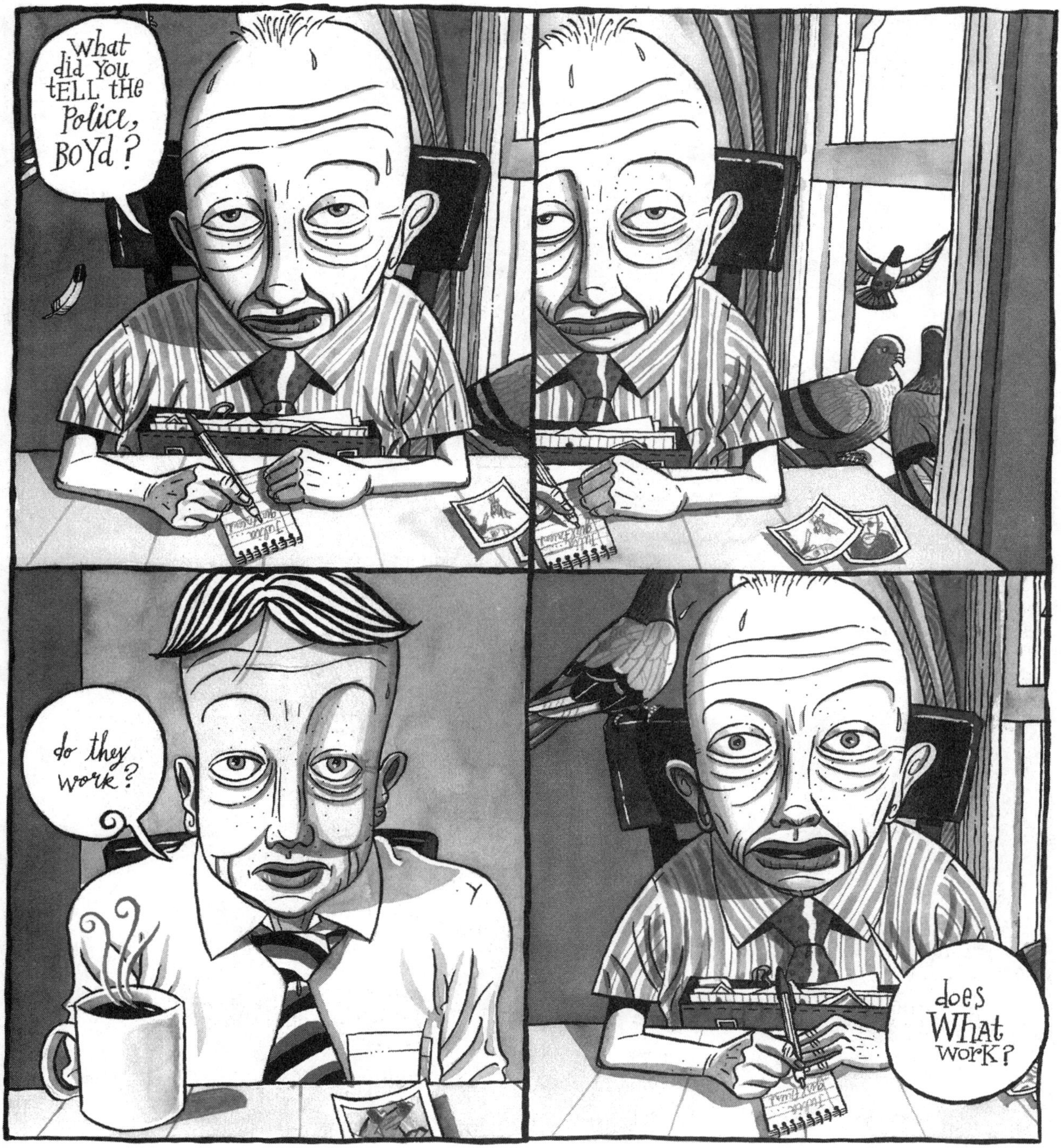
What did You tELL tHe Police, BOYd?
do they work?
does What work?

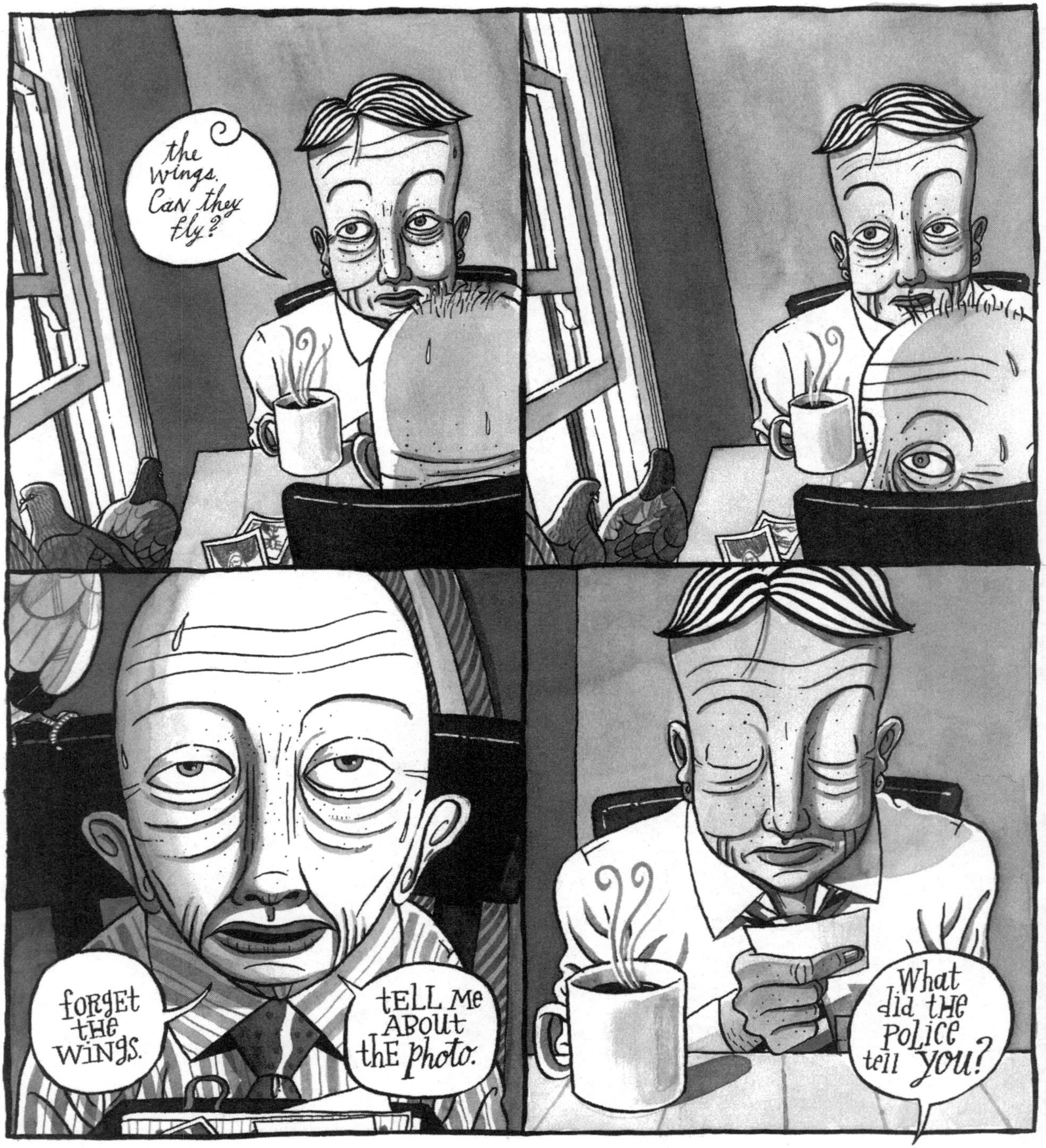
the wings. Can they fly?
forget the wings.
tell me about the photo.
What did the police tell you?

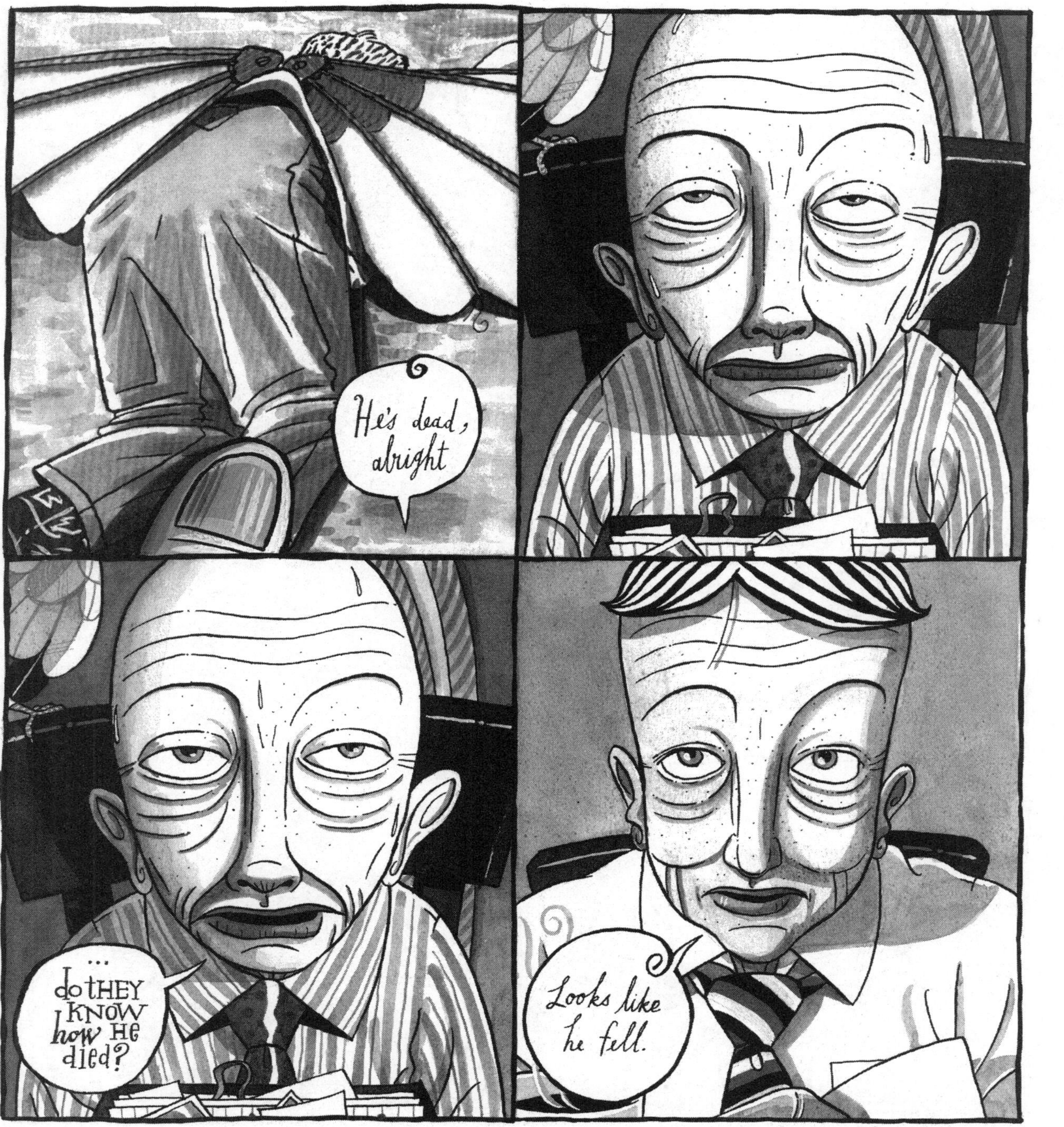
He's dead, alright
... do THEY KNOW how HE died?
Looks like he fell.

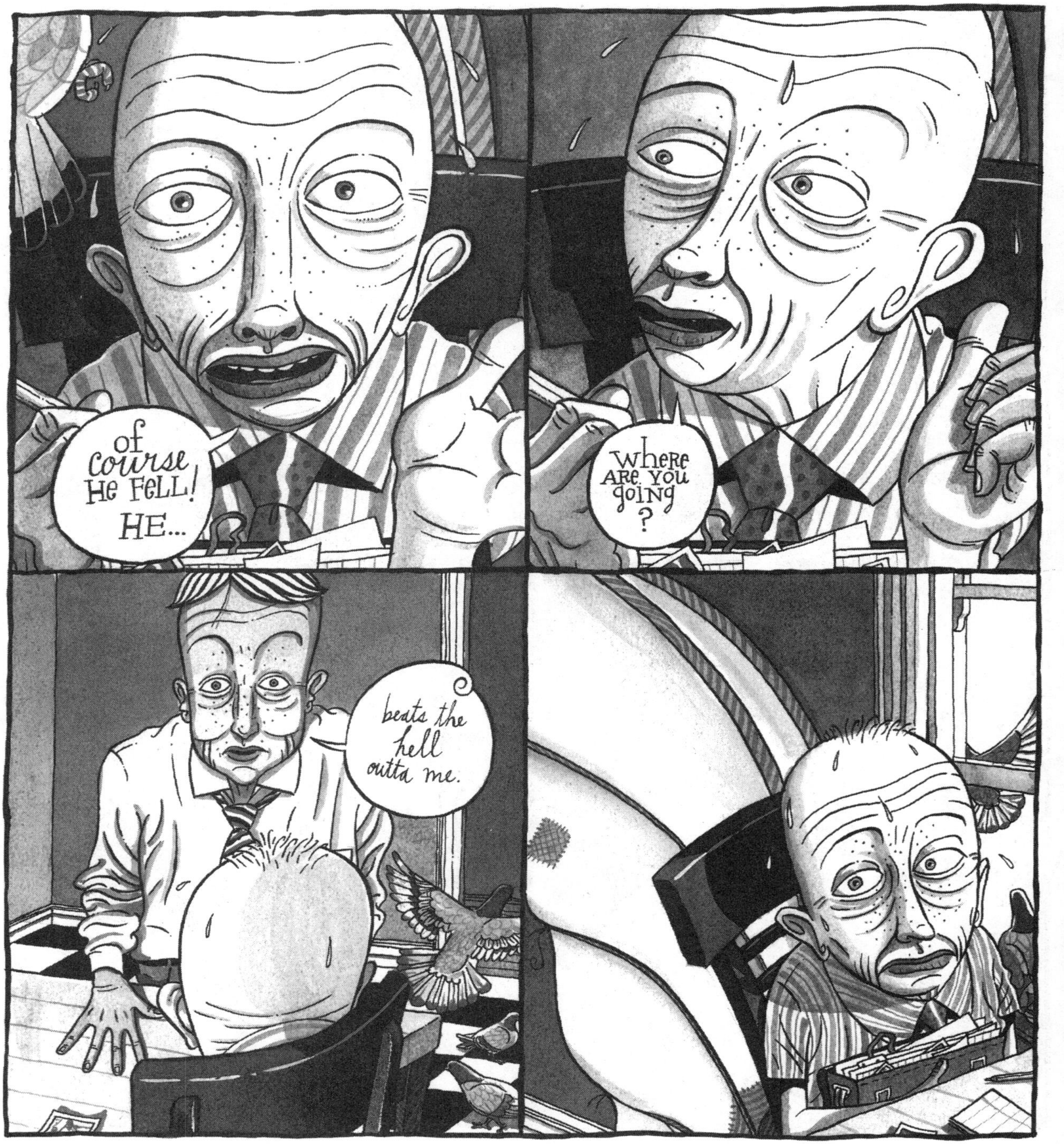
of course He FeLL! HE...
Where ARE YOU going?
beats the hell outta me.

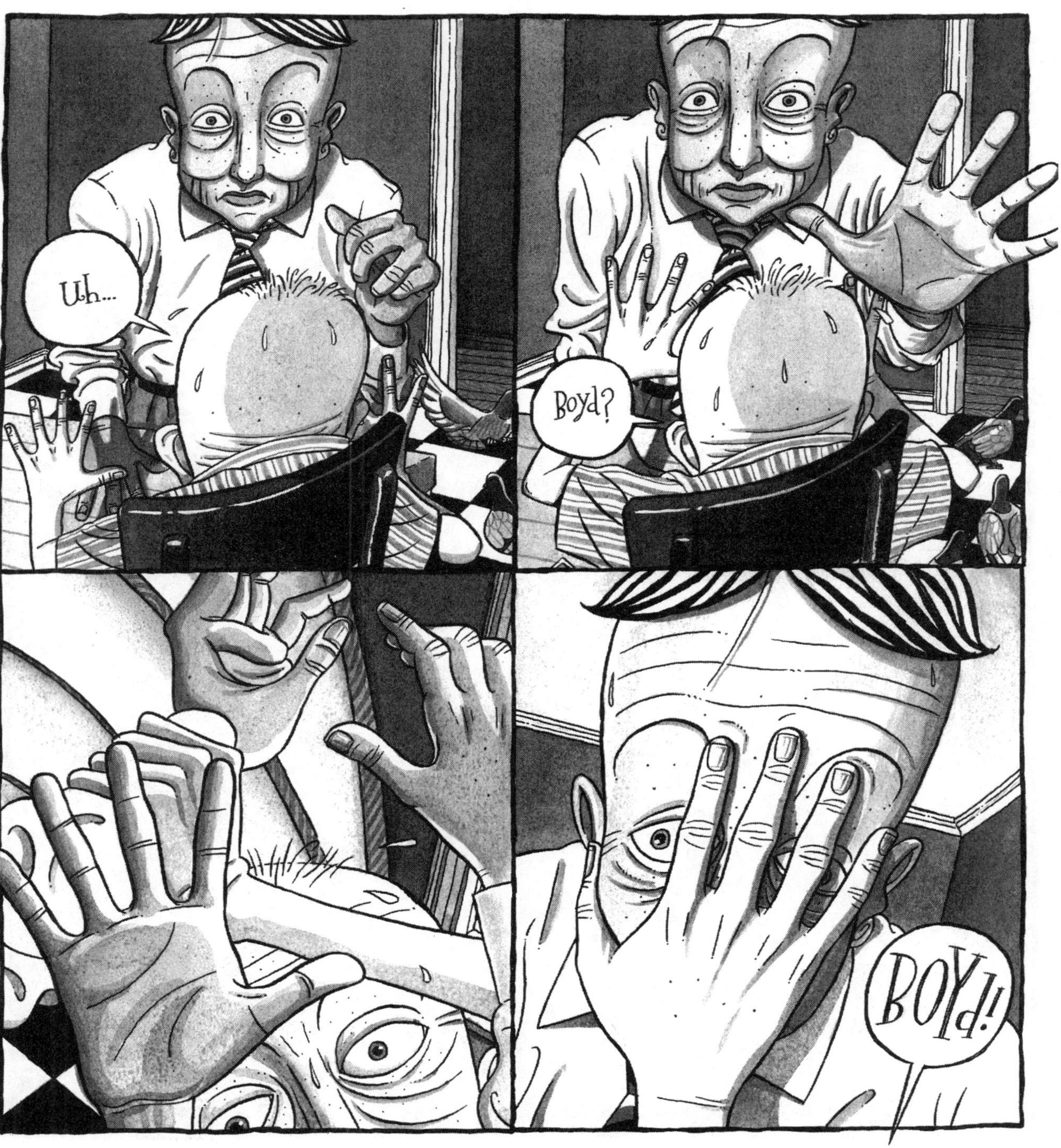

Uh...
Boyd?
BOYd!

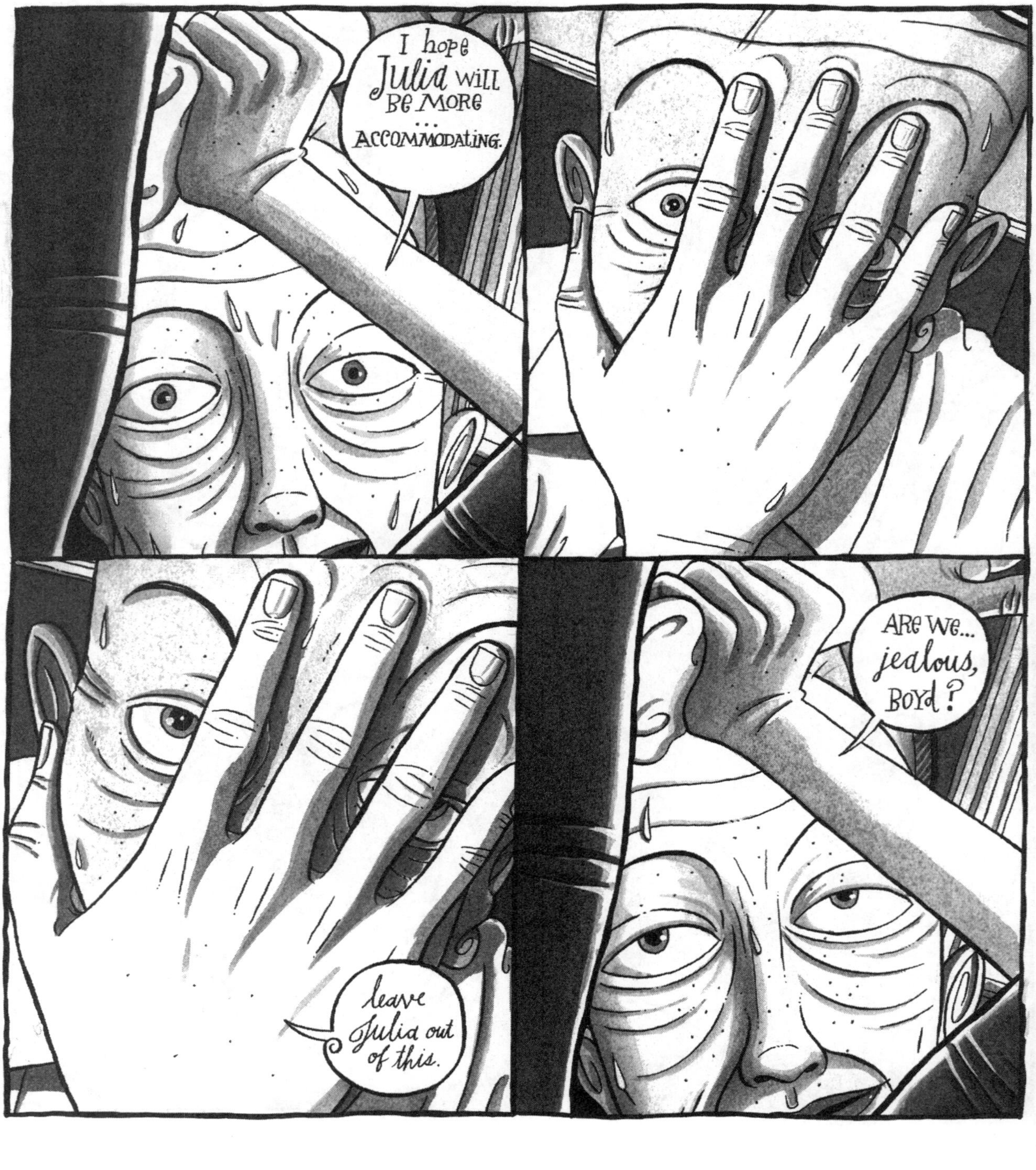

I hope Julia will be more ... accommodating.
leave Julia out of this.
Are we... jealous, Boyd?

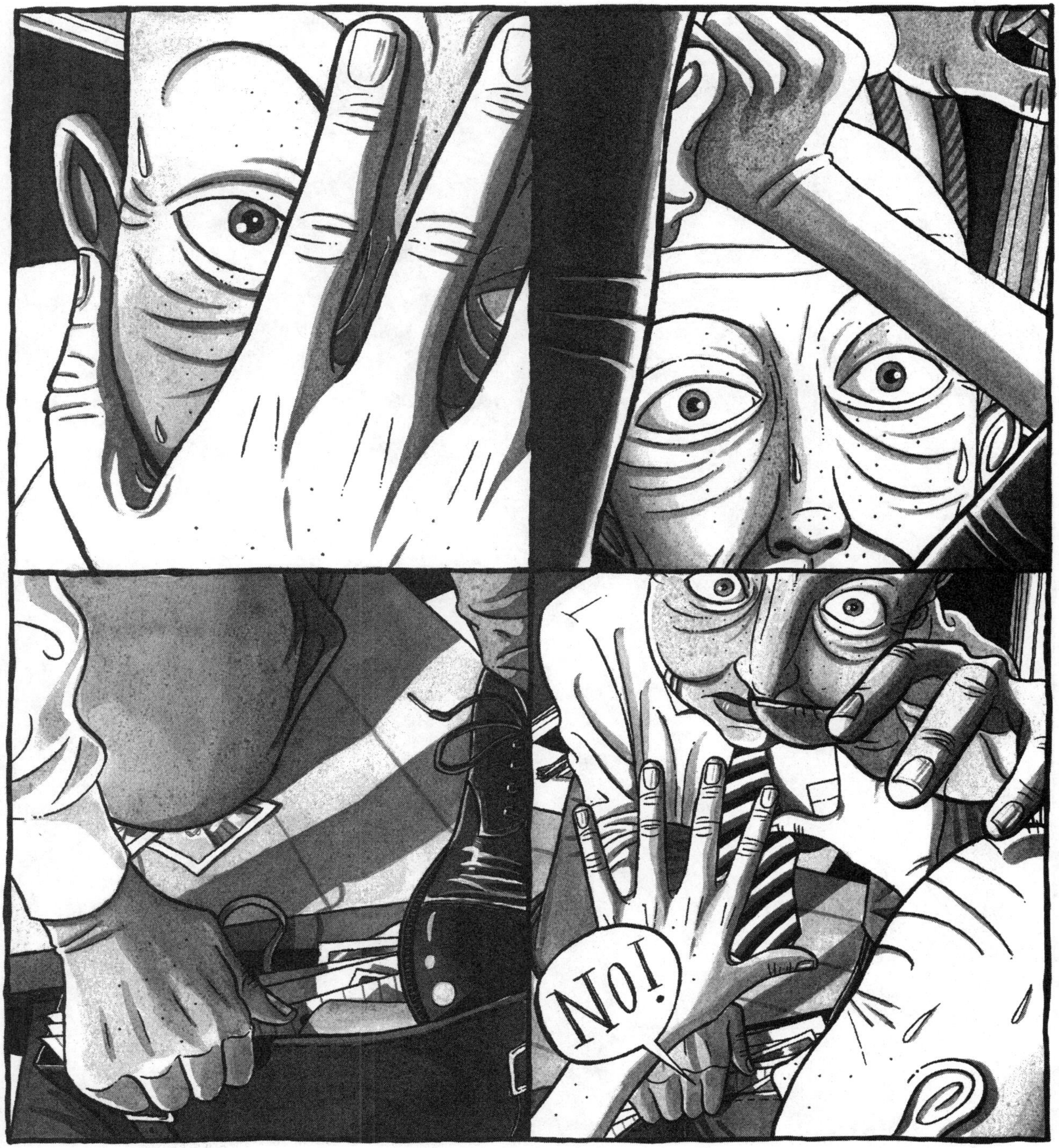
NO!

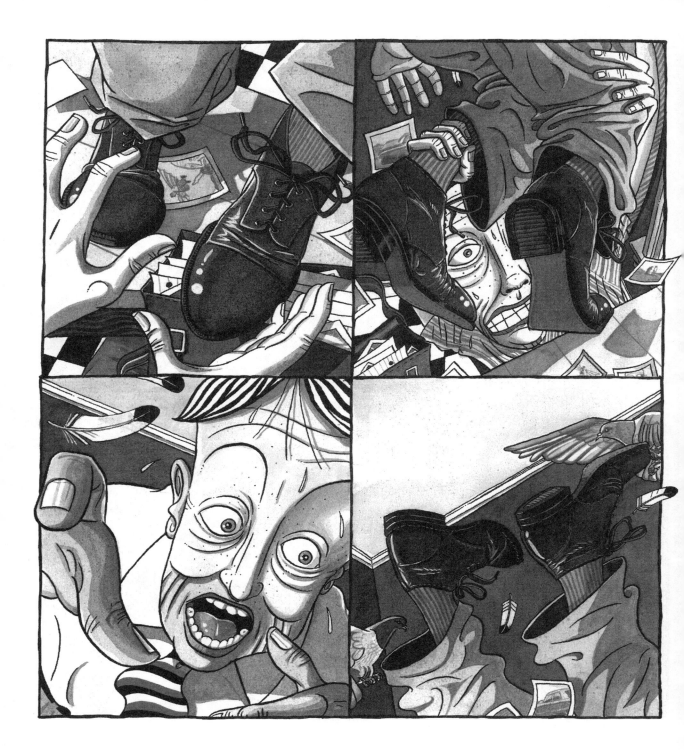

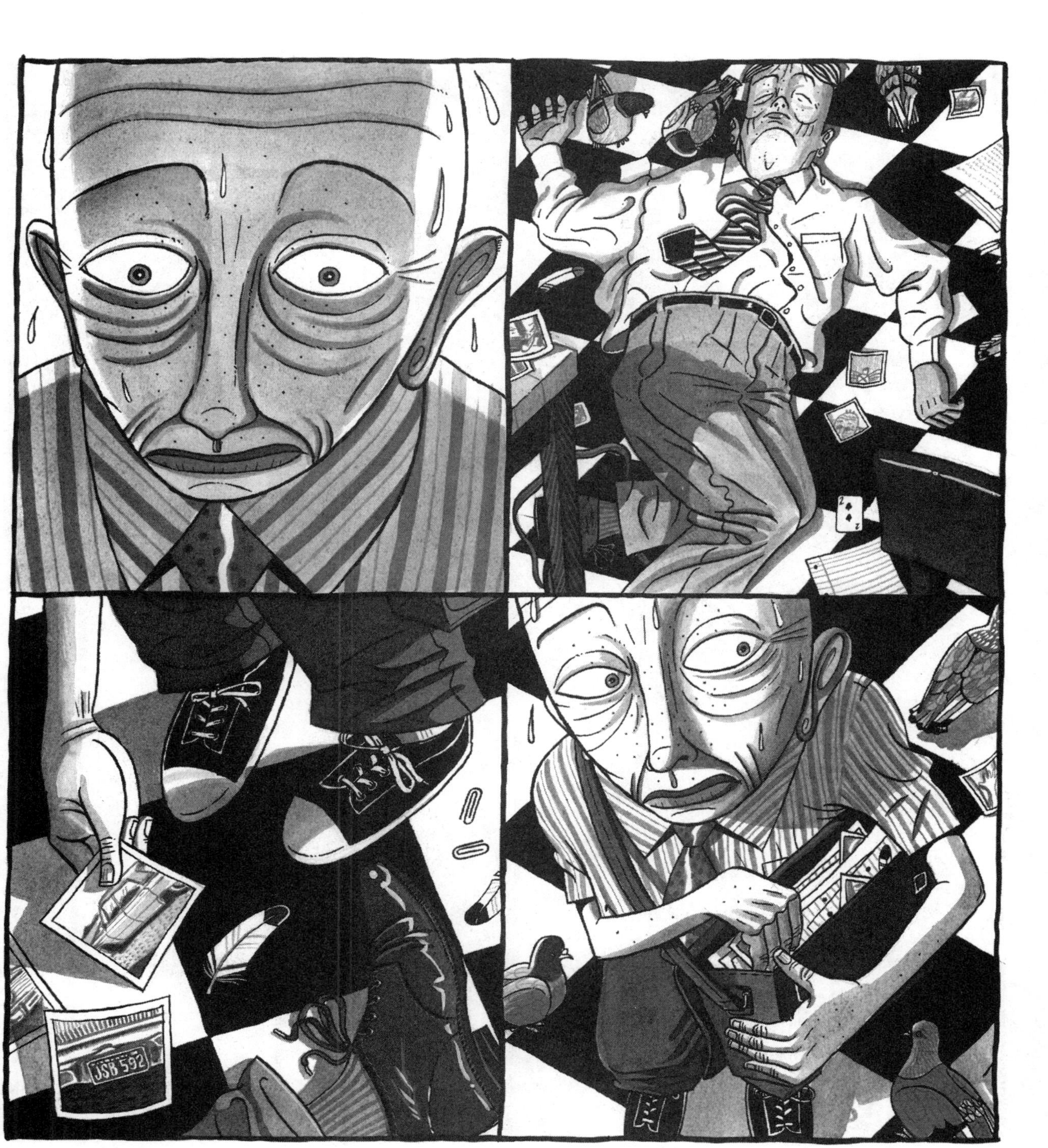
JSB 592

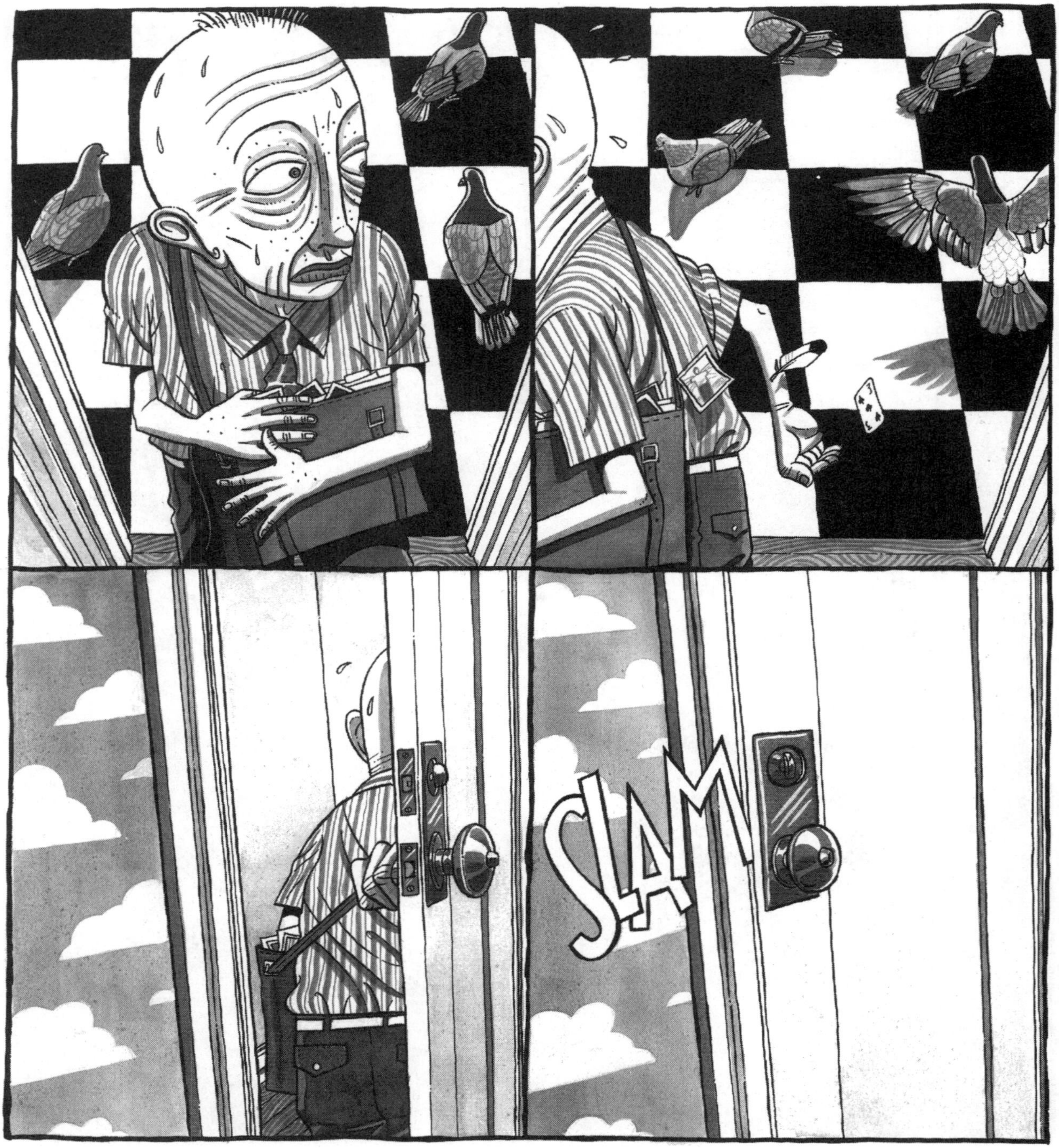
SLAM

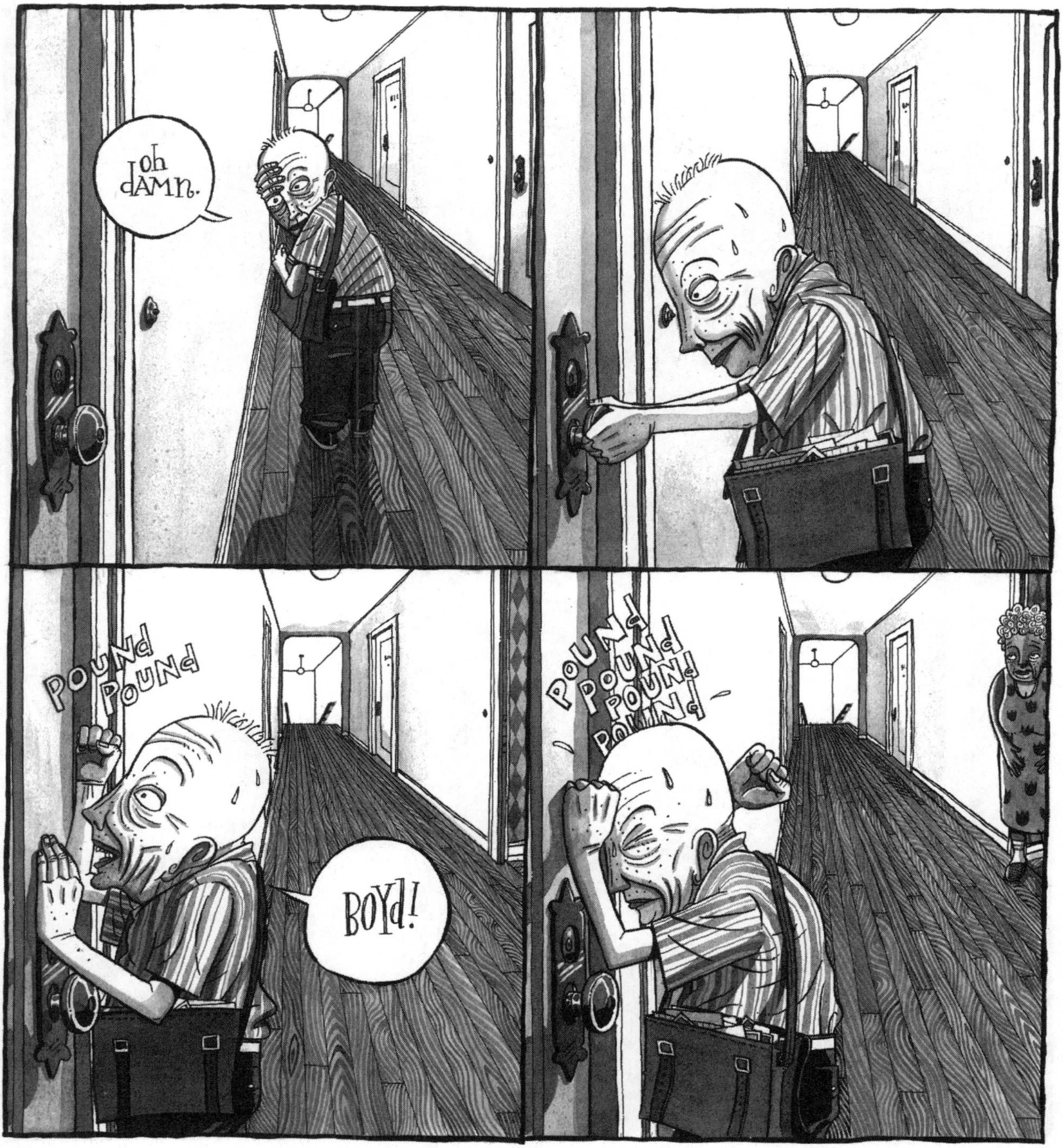
oh damn.
POUND POUND
BOYD!
POUND POUND POUND POUND

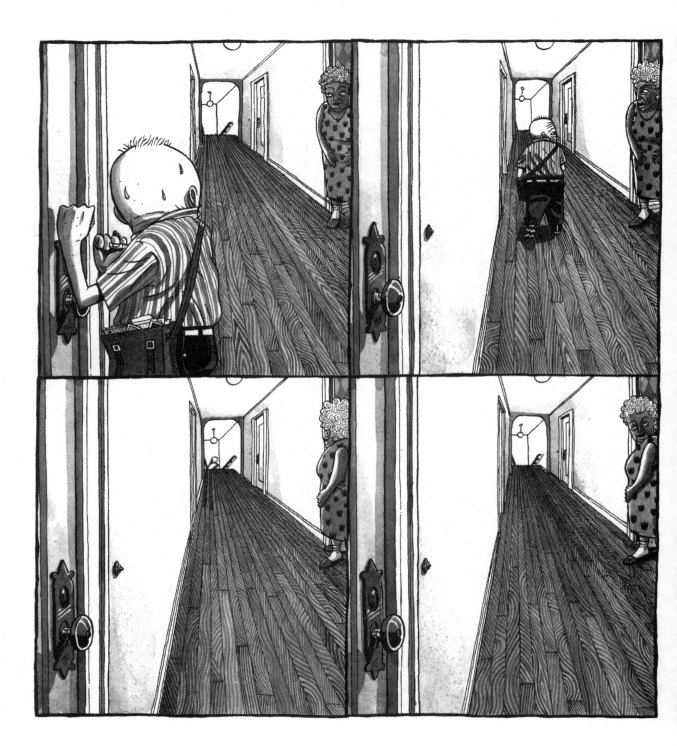

four

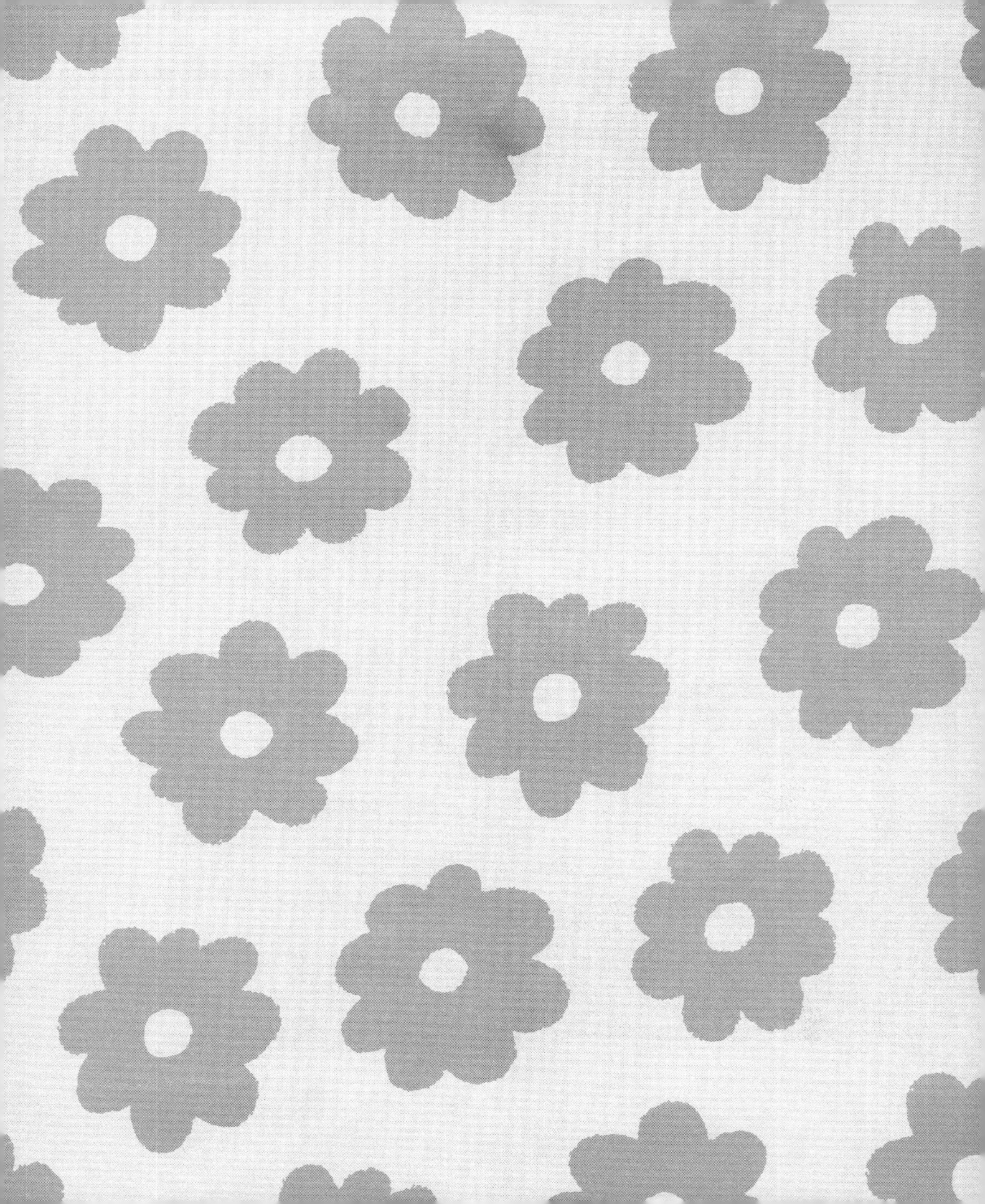

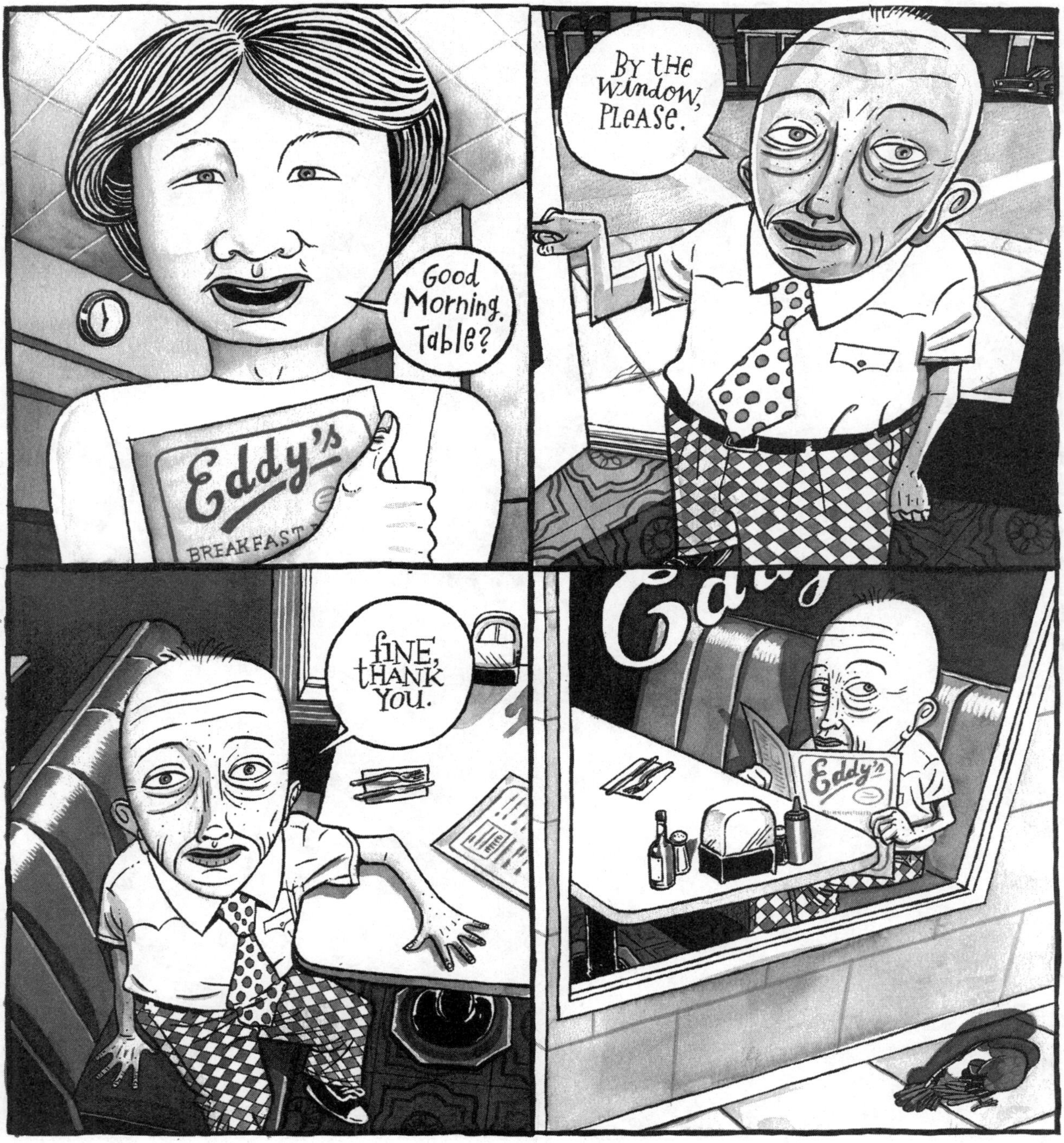
Good Morning. Table?
Eddy's
BREAKFAST
By the window, please.
fine, thank you.
Eddy's

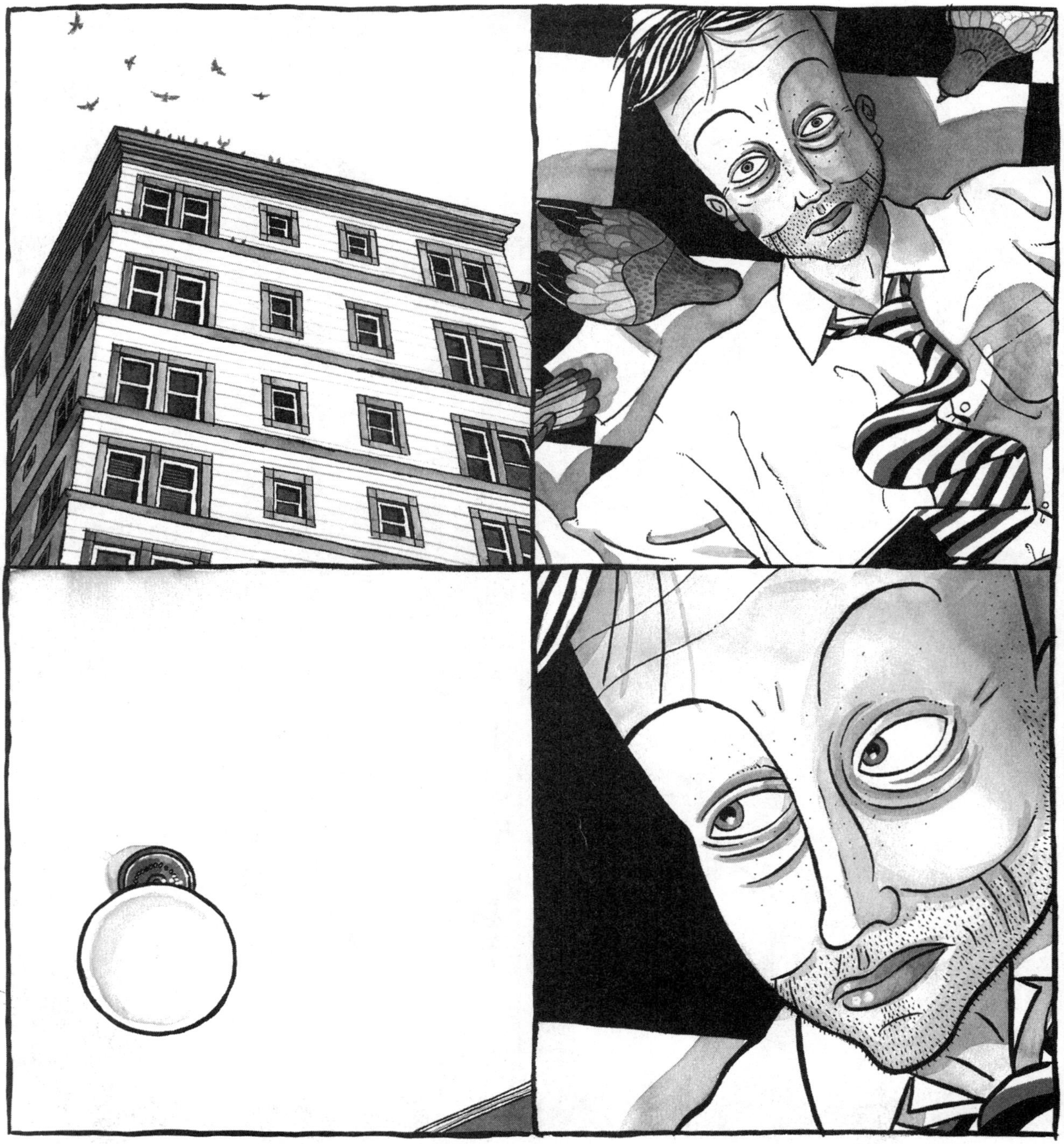

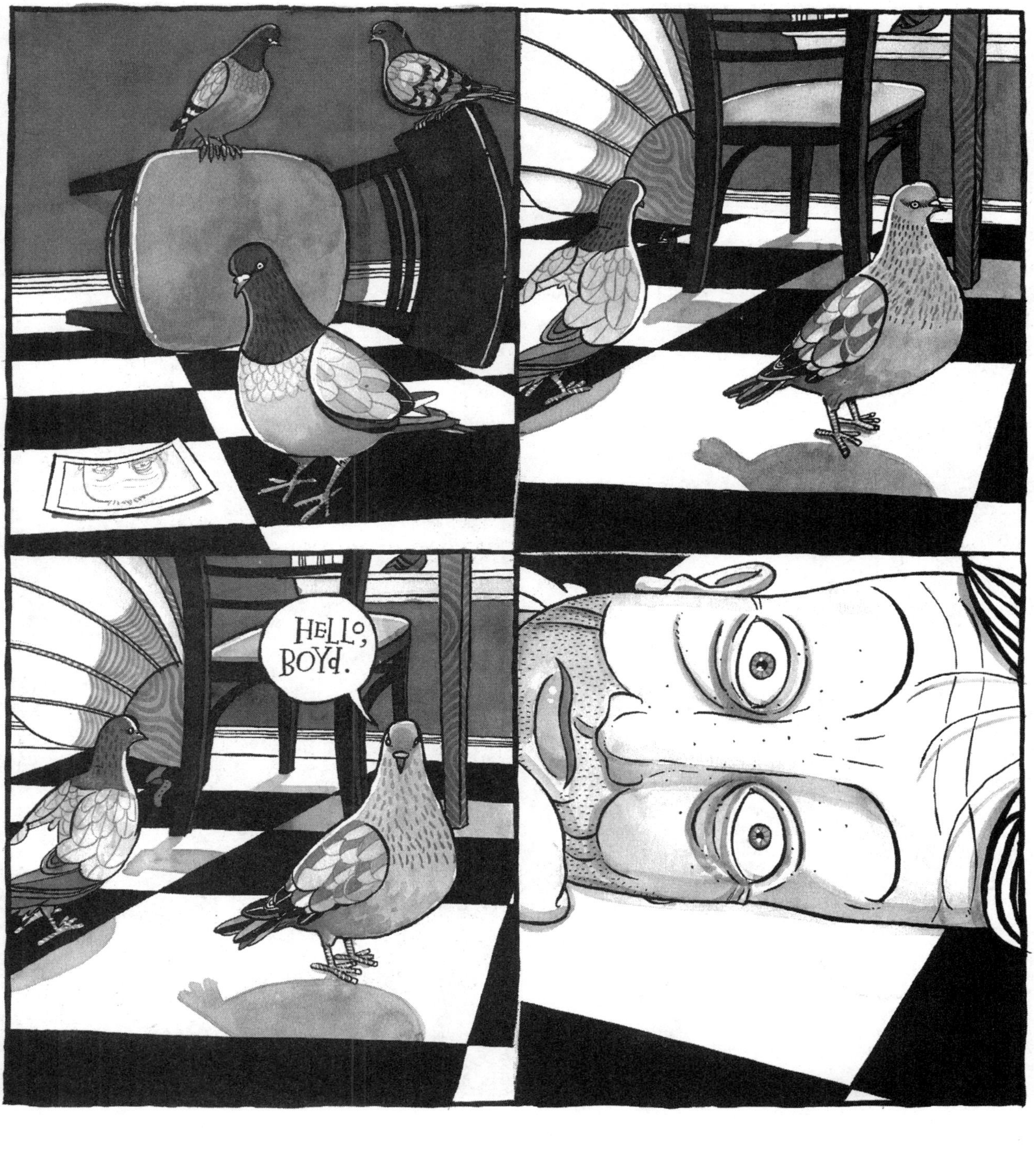
HELLO, BOYD.

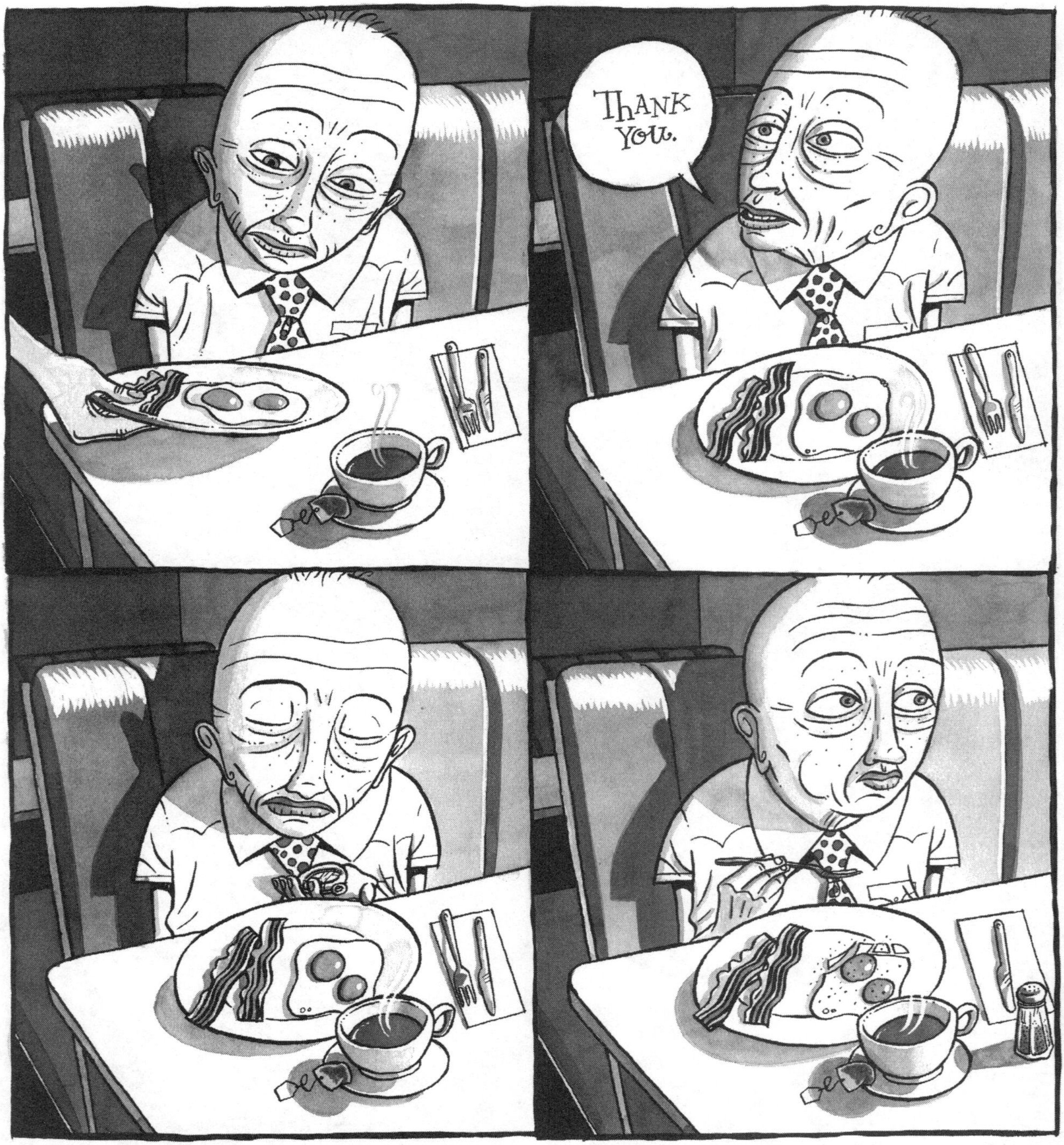
THANK YOU.

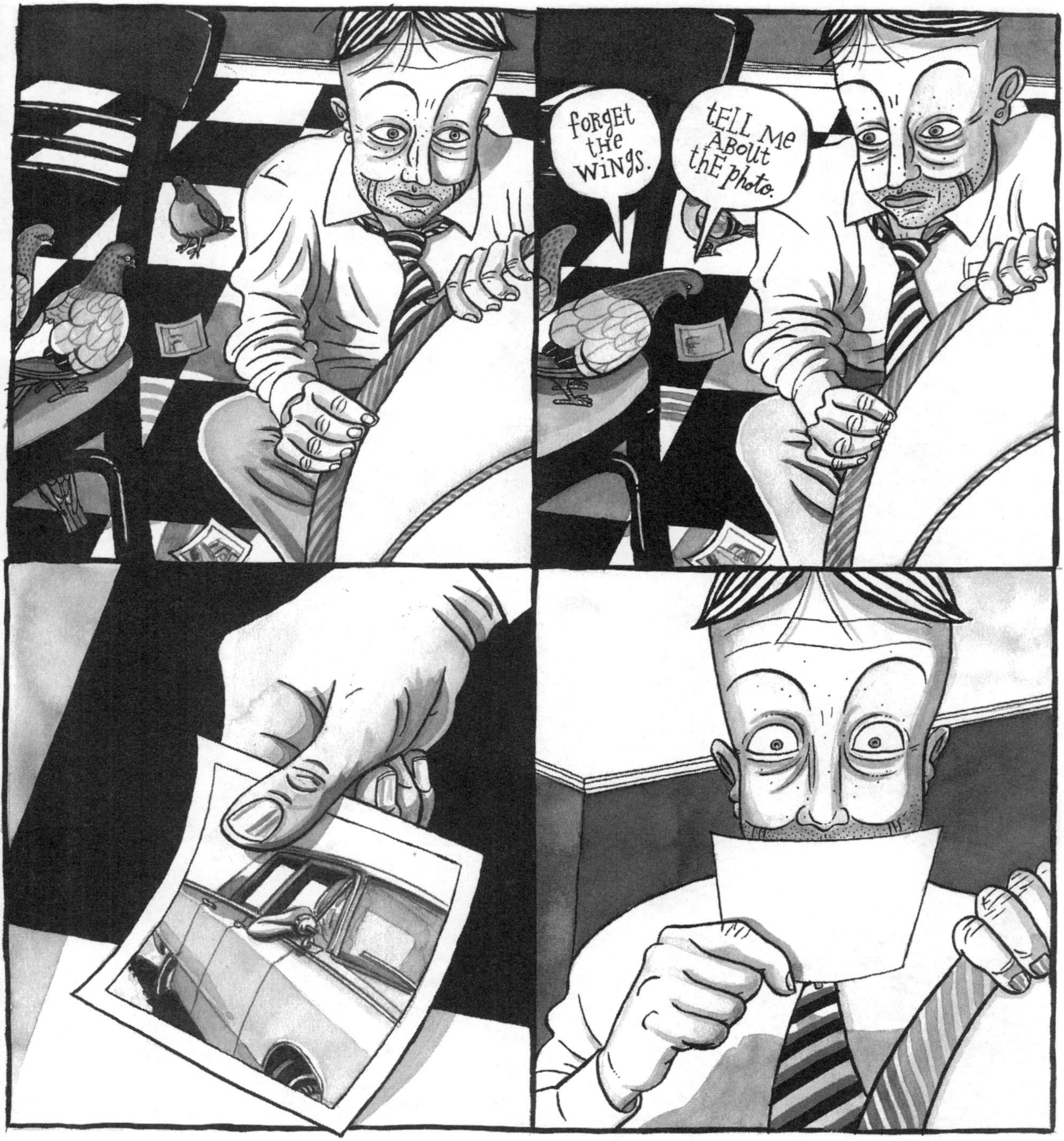
forget the wings.
tell me about the photo.

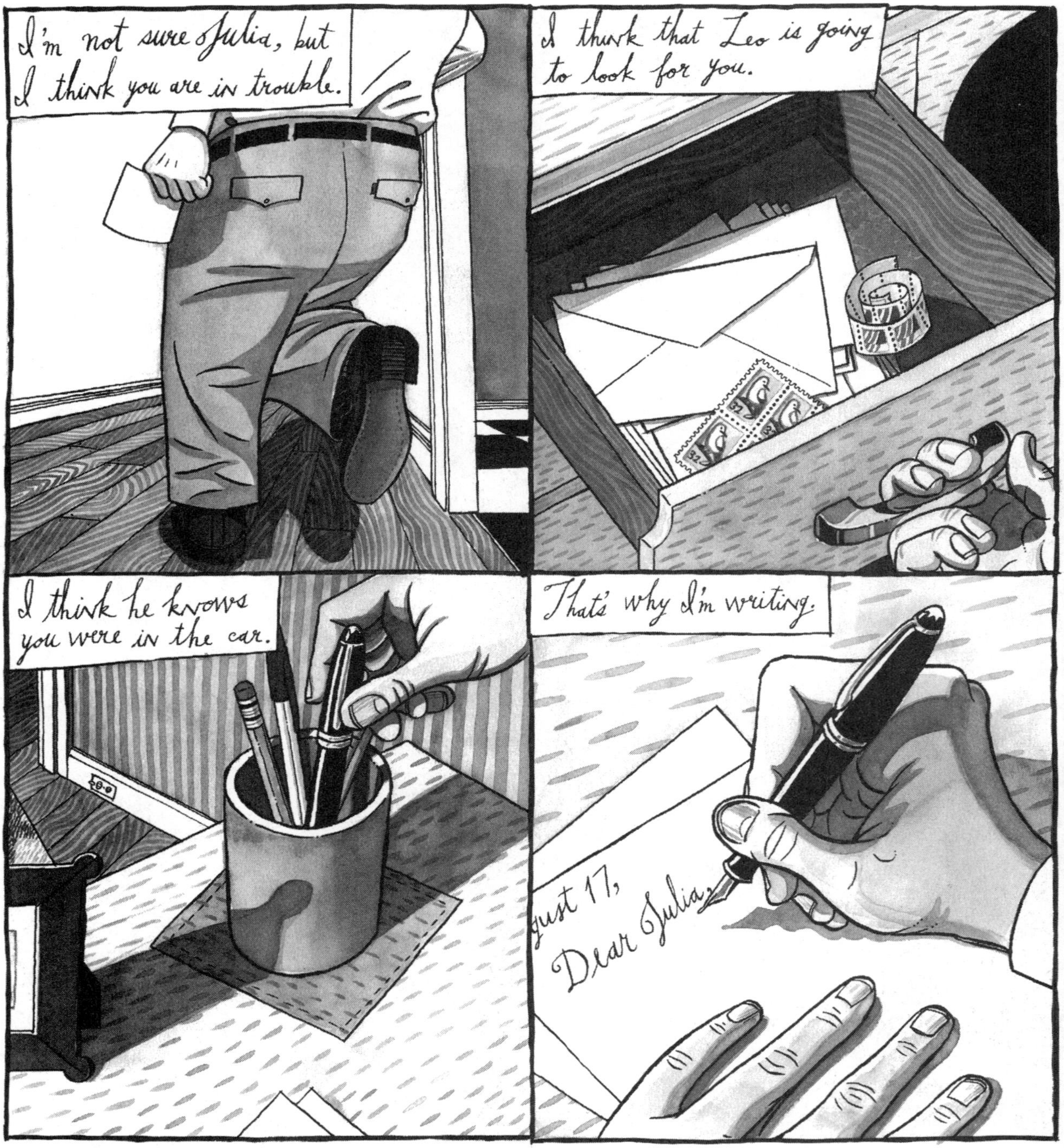

I'm not sure Julia, but I think you are in trouble.
I think that Leo is going to look for you.
I think he knows you were in the car.
That's why I'm writing.
just 17,
Dear Julia,

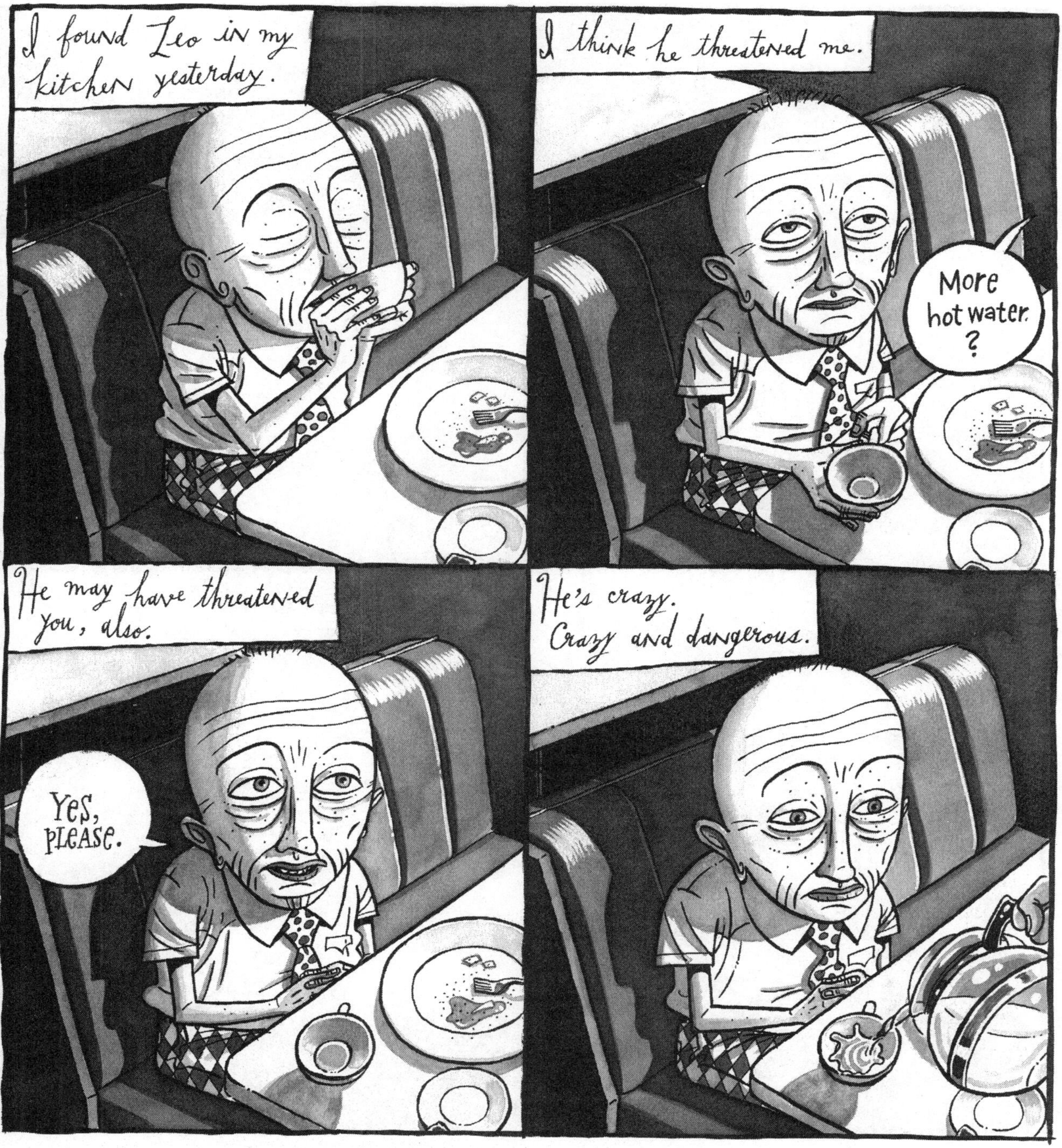
I found Leo in my kitchen yesterday.
I think he threatened me.
More hot water.
?
He may have threatened you, also.
Yes, please.
He's crazy.
Crazy and dangerous.

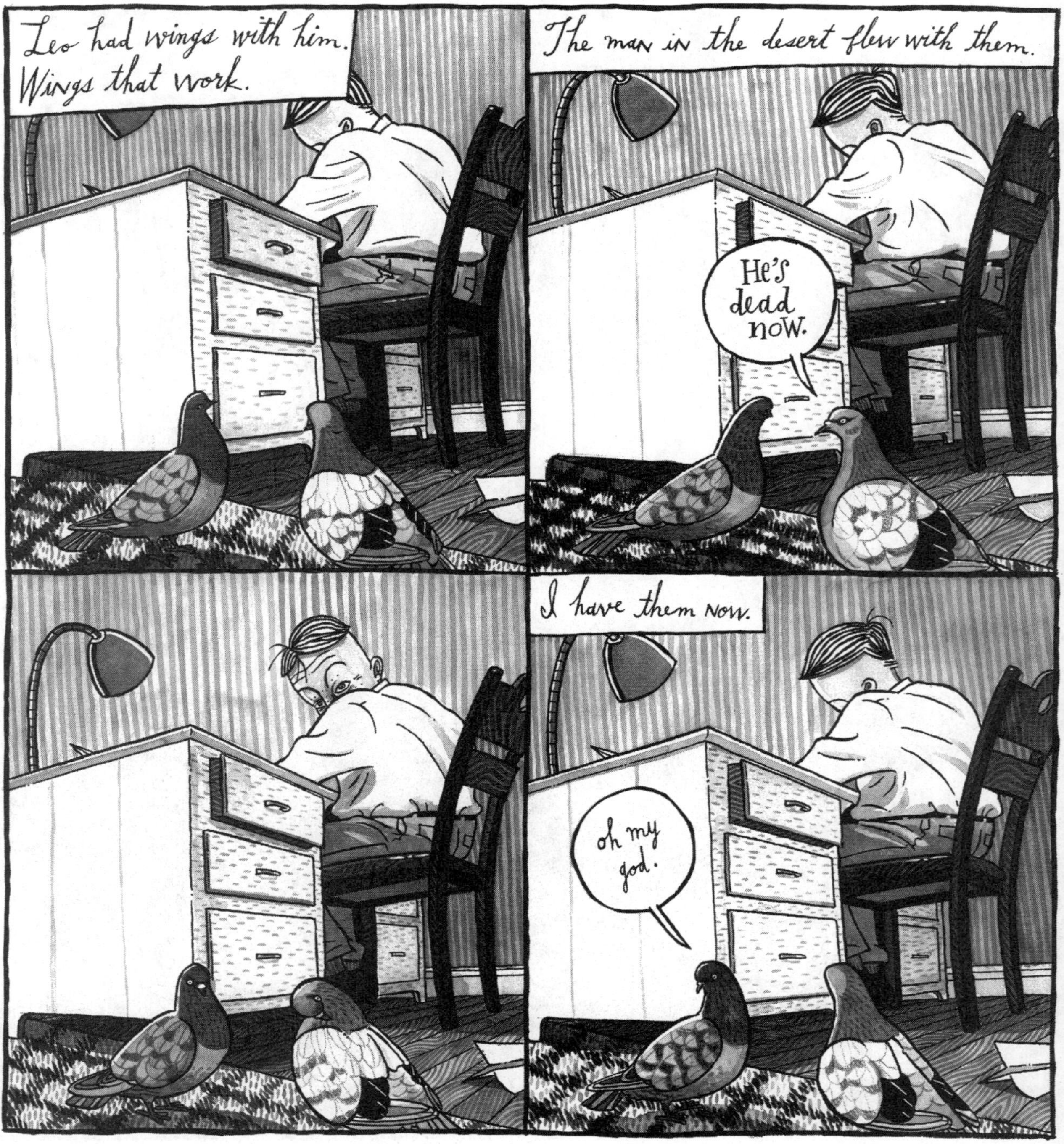
Leo had wings with him. Wings that work.
The man in the desert flew with them.
He's dead now.
I have them now.
oh my god!

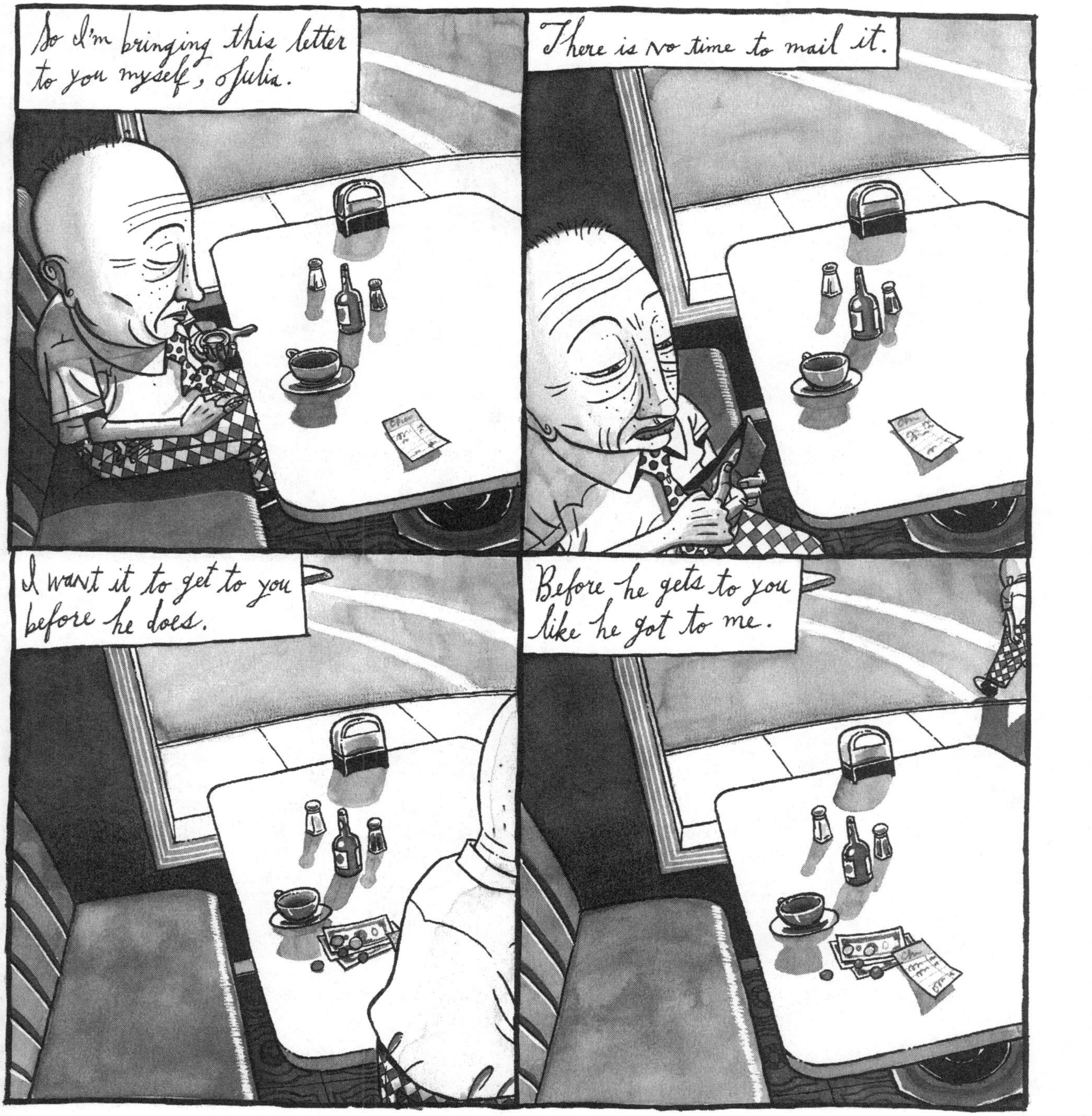
So I'm bringing this letter to you myself, Julia.
There is no time to mail it.
I want it to get to you before he does.
Before he gets to you like he got to me.

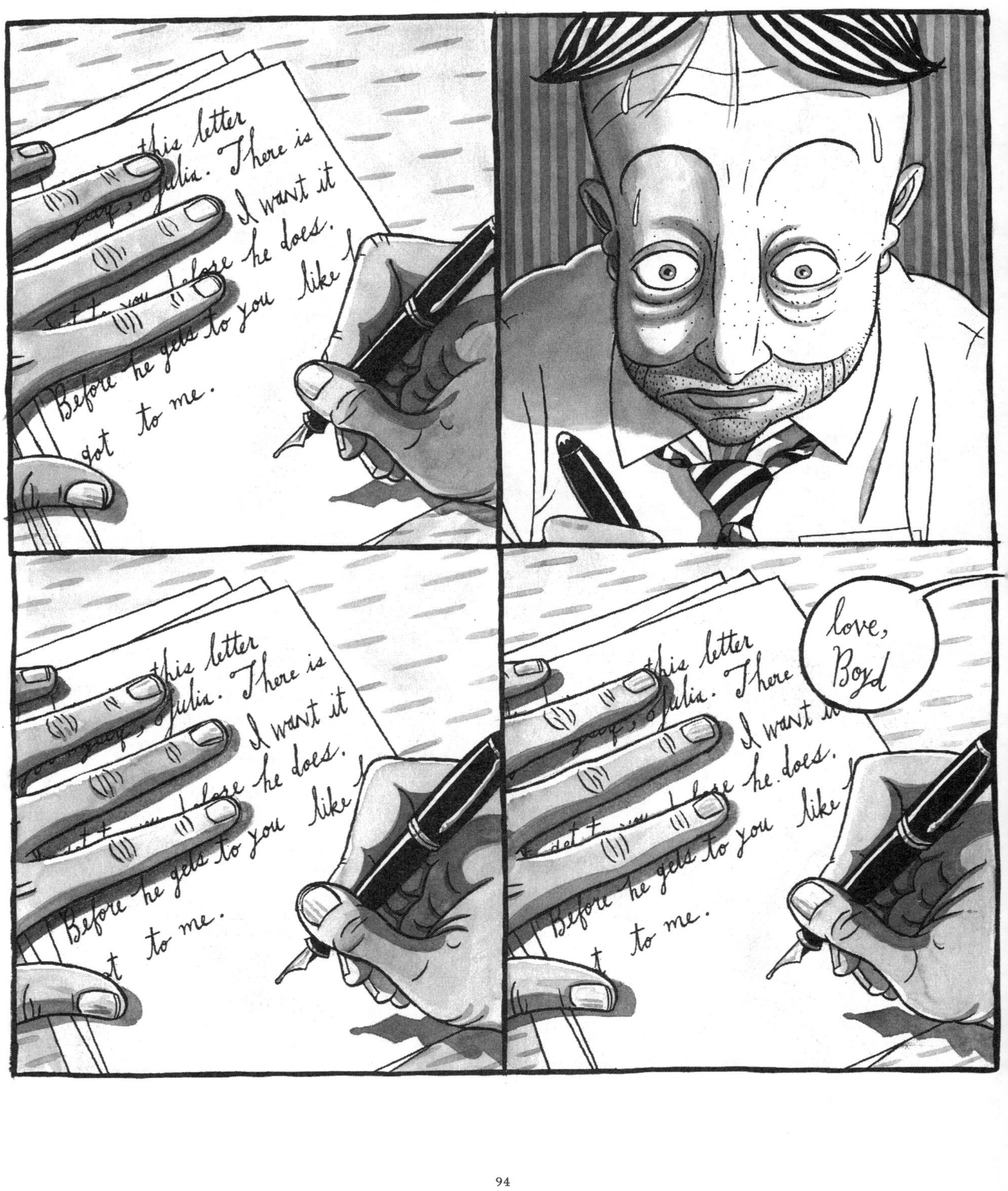
this letter
Julia. There is
I want it
he does.
Before he gets to you like
got to me.
love,
Boyd

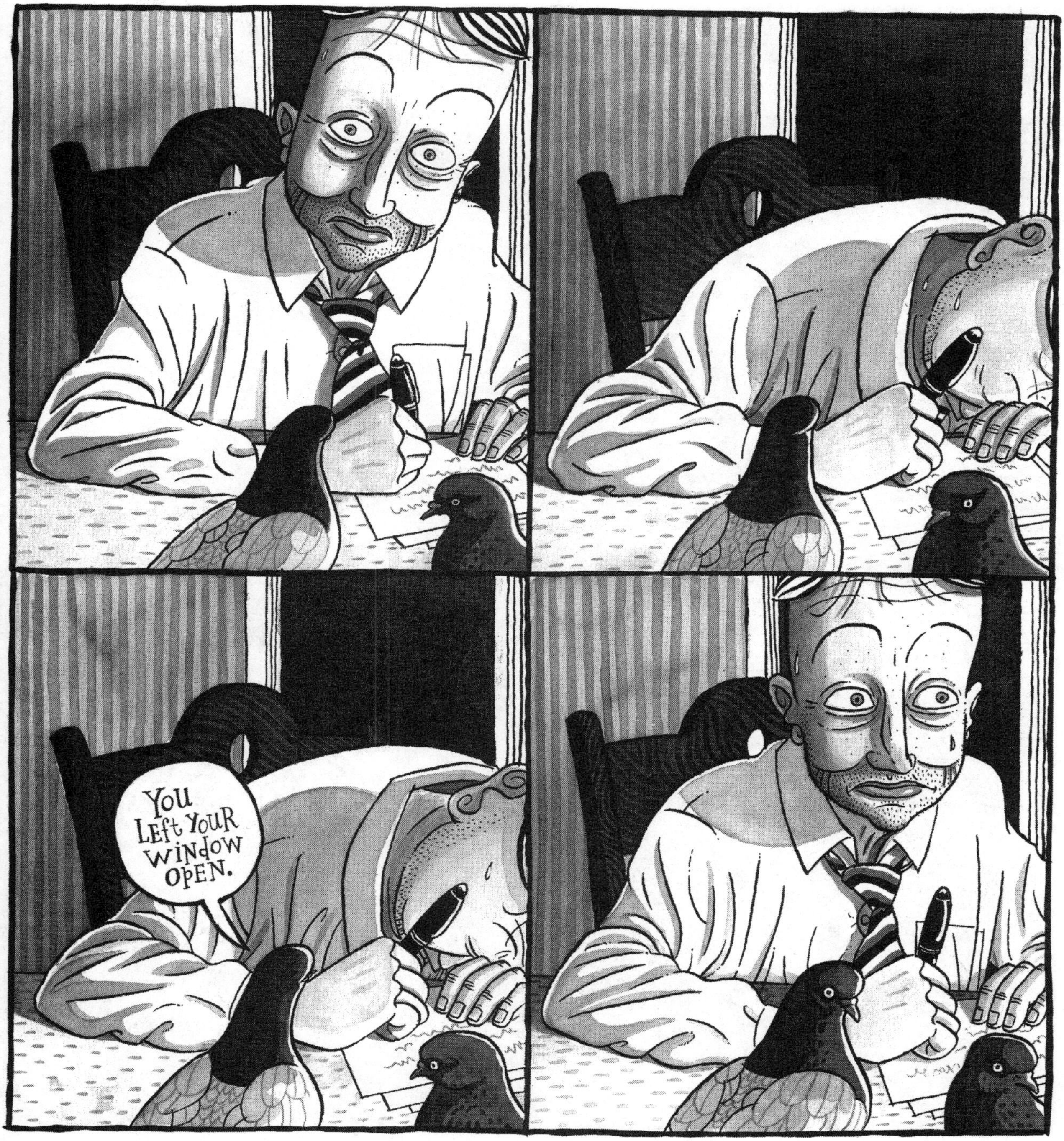
YOU LEFT YOUR WINDOW OPEN.

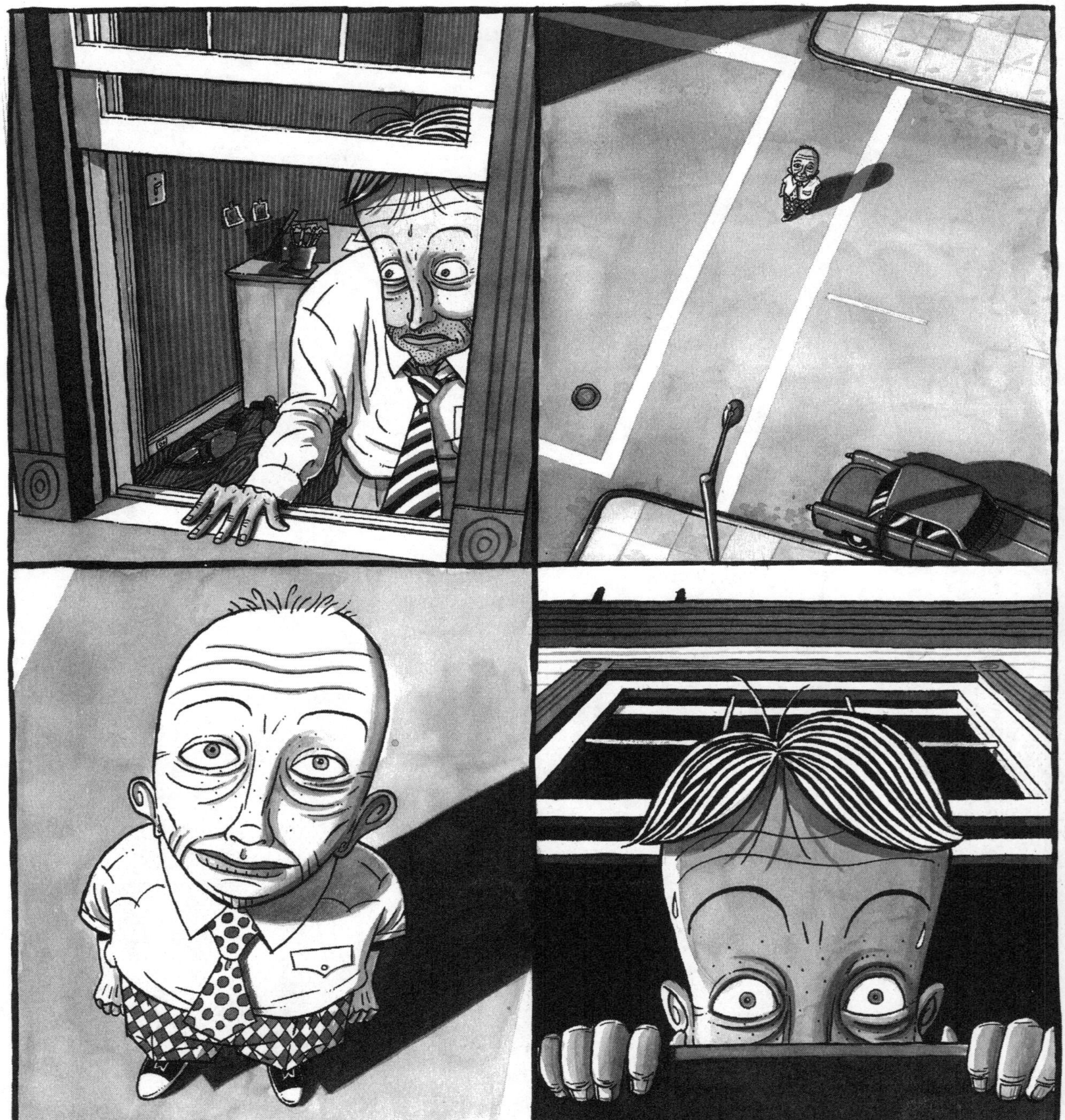

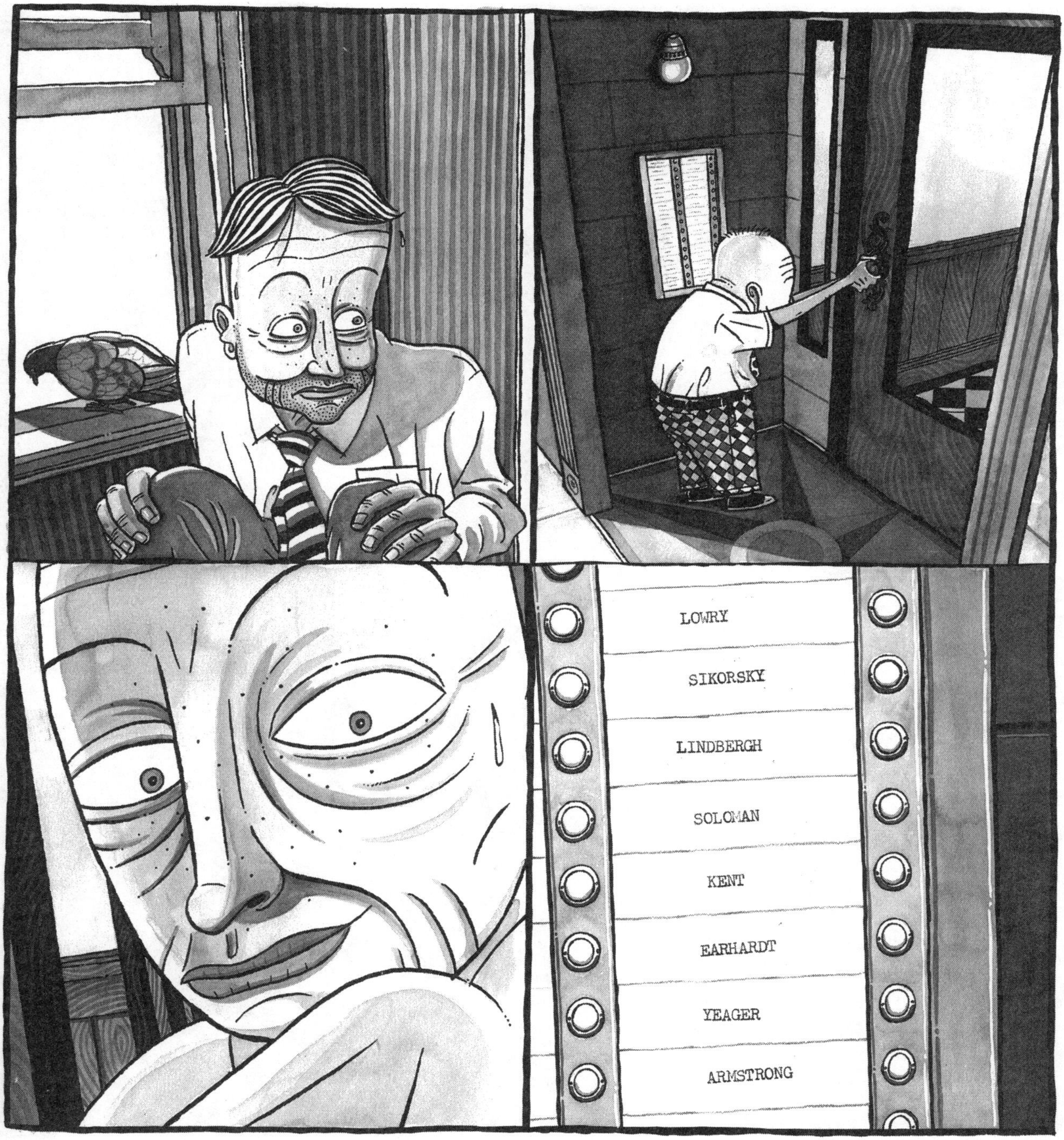
LOWRY
SIKORSKY
LINDBERGH
SOLOMAN
KENT
EARHARDT
YEAGER
ARMSTRONG

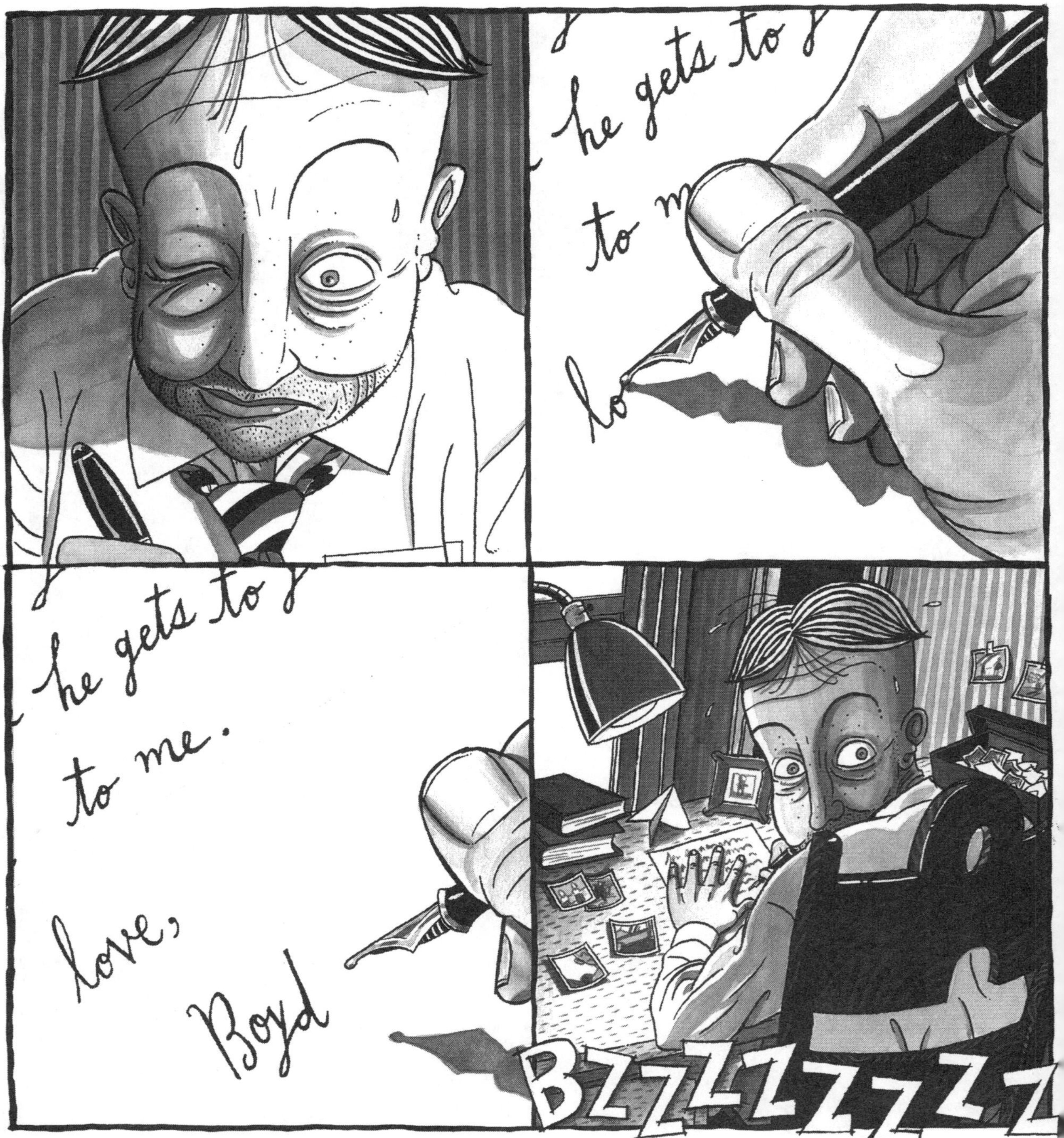
he gets to
to m
lo
he gets to
to me.
love,
Boyd
BZZZZZZZZ

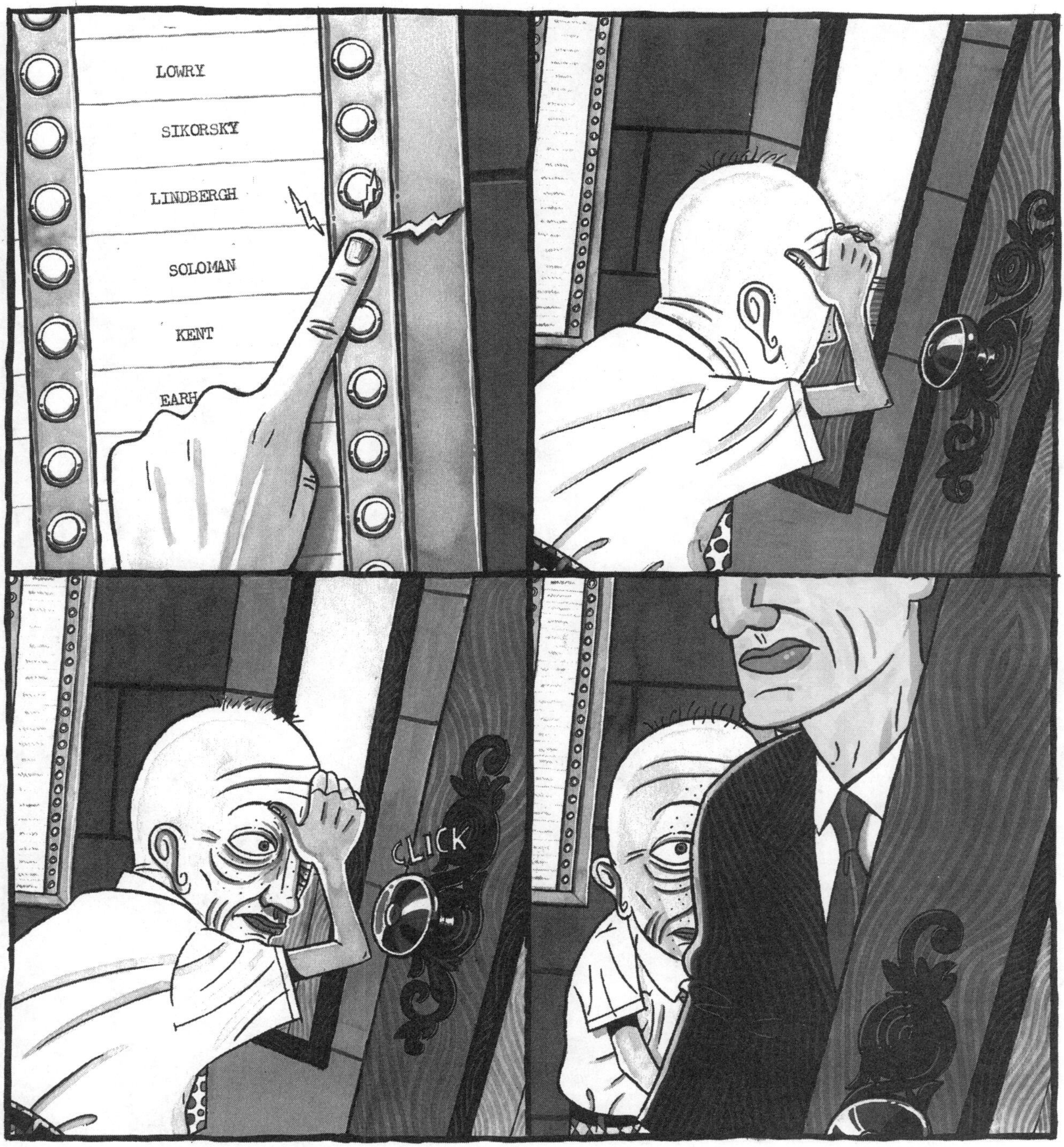
LOWRY
SIKORSKY
LINDBERGH
SOLOMAN
KENT
EARH
CLICK

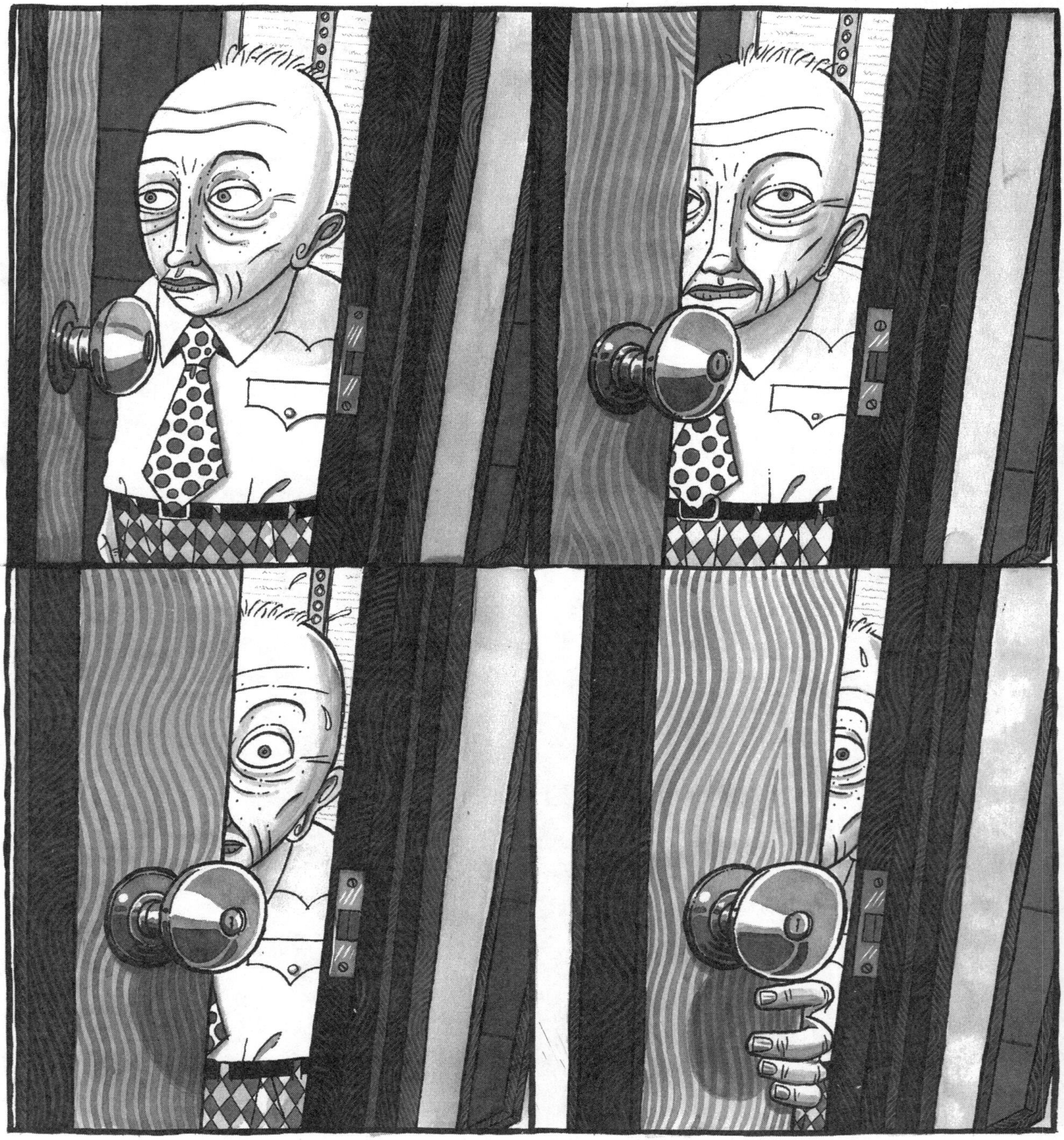

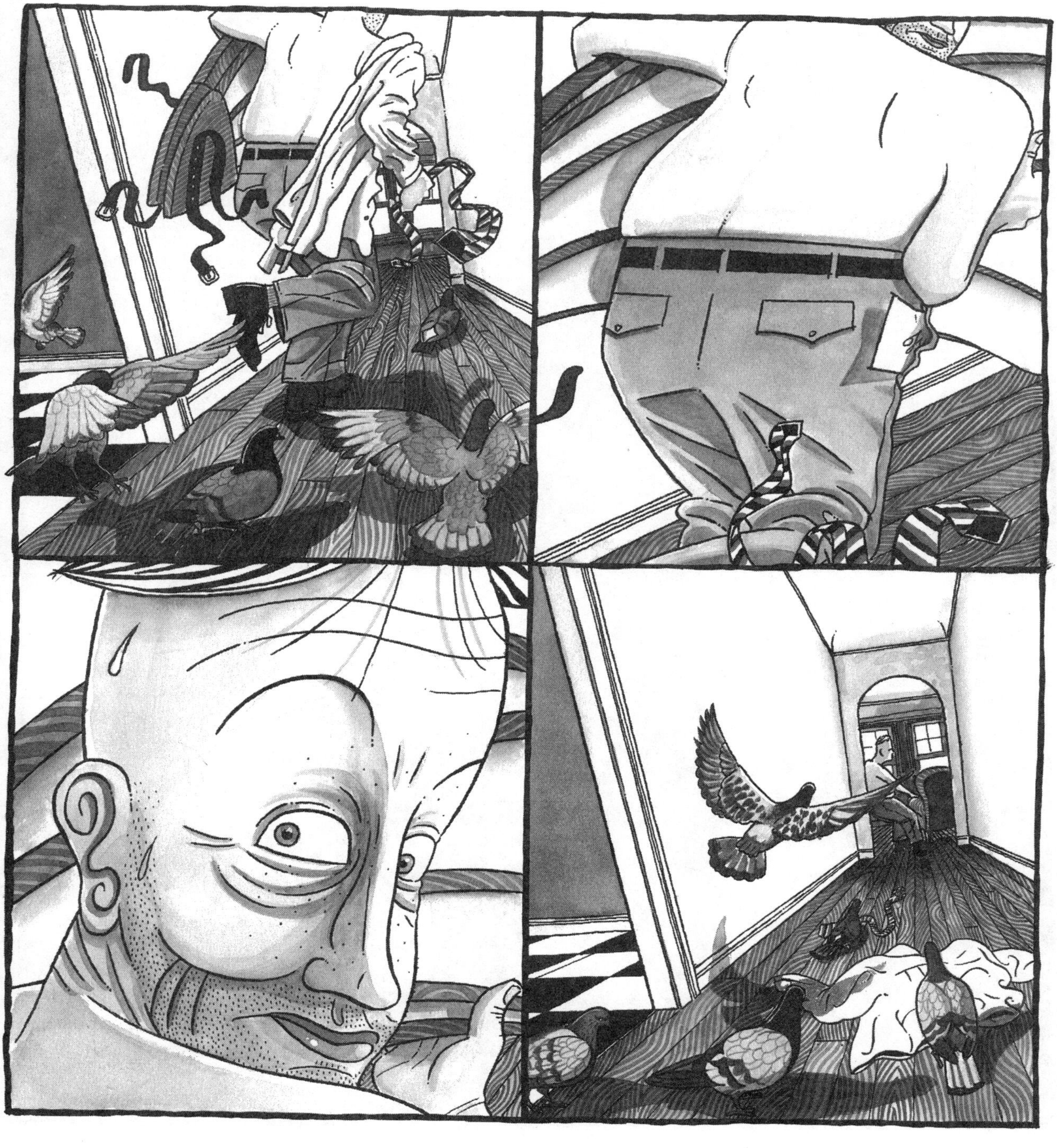

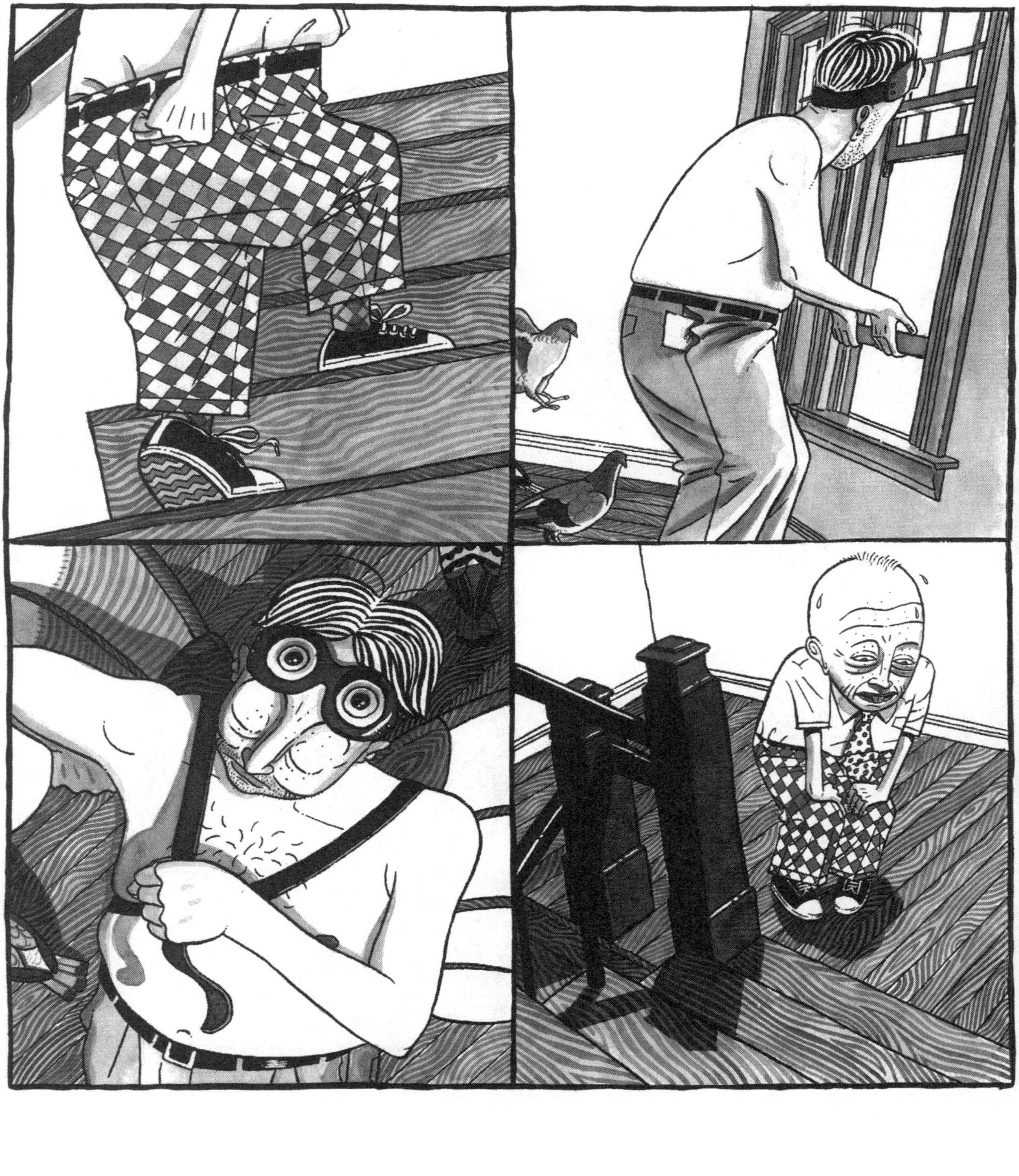

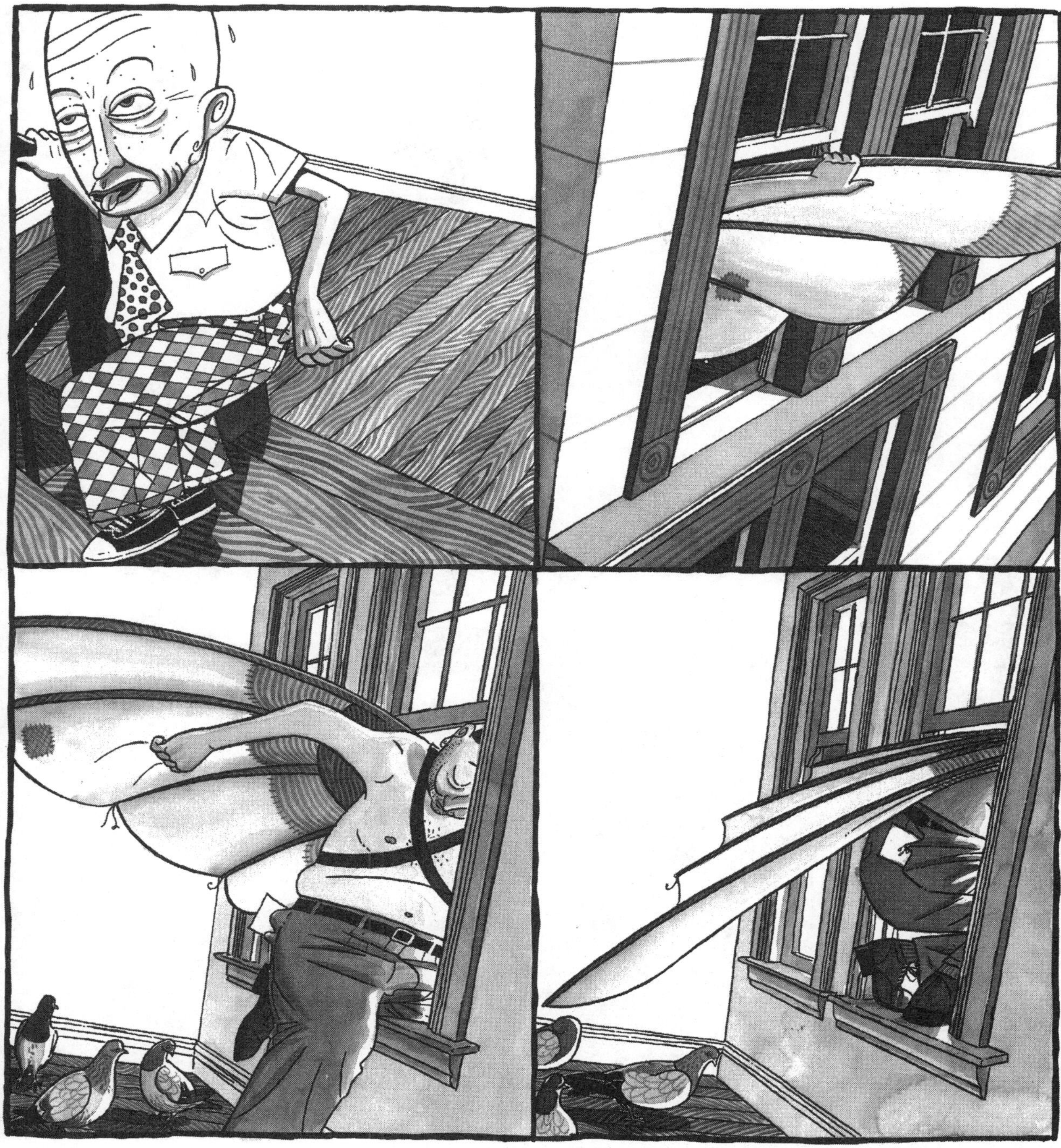

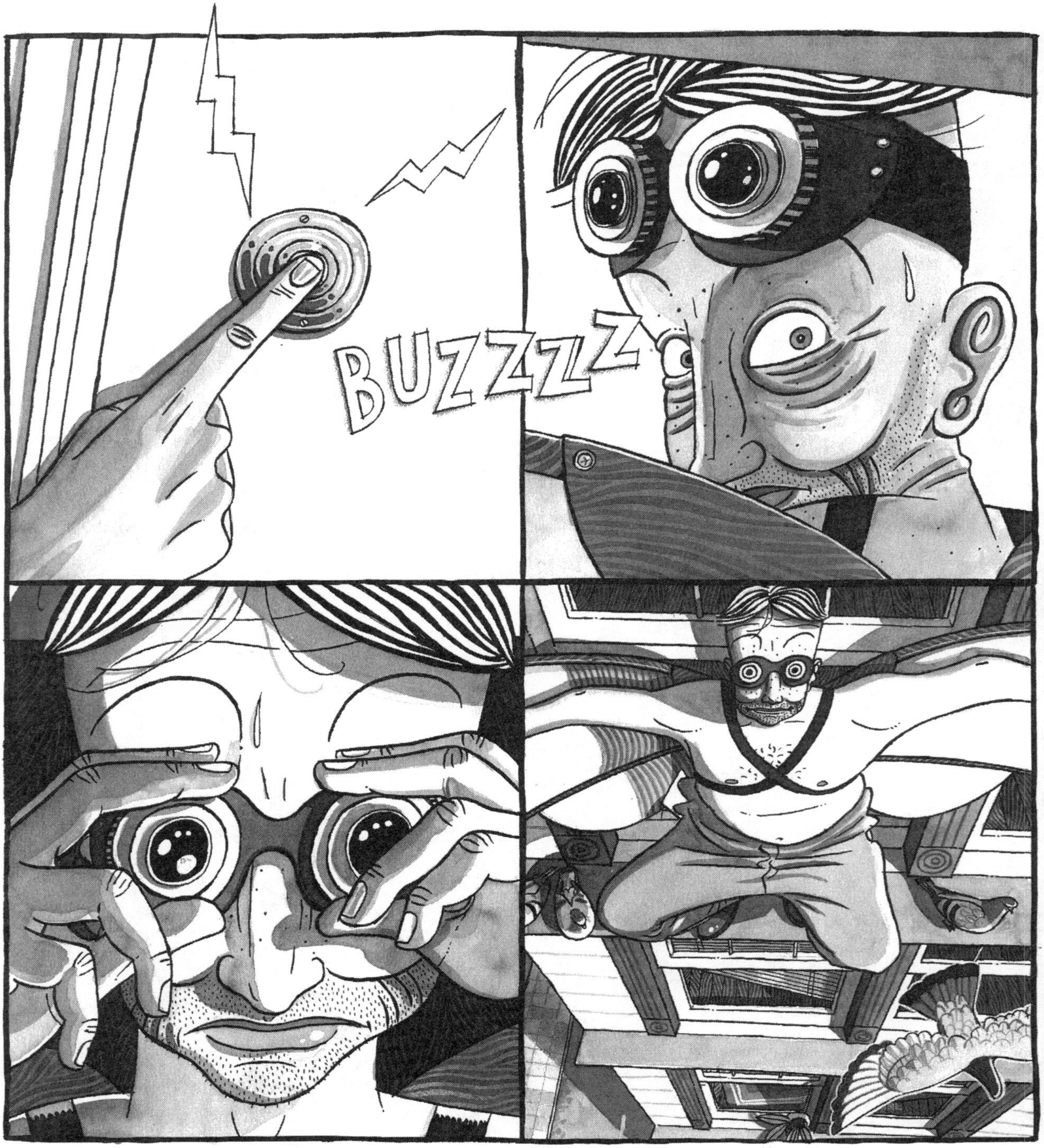
BUZZZZZ

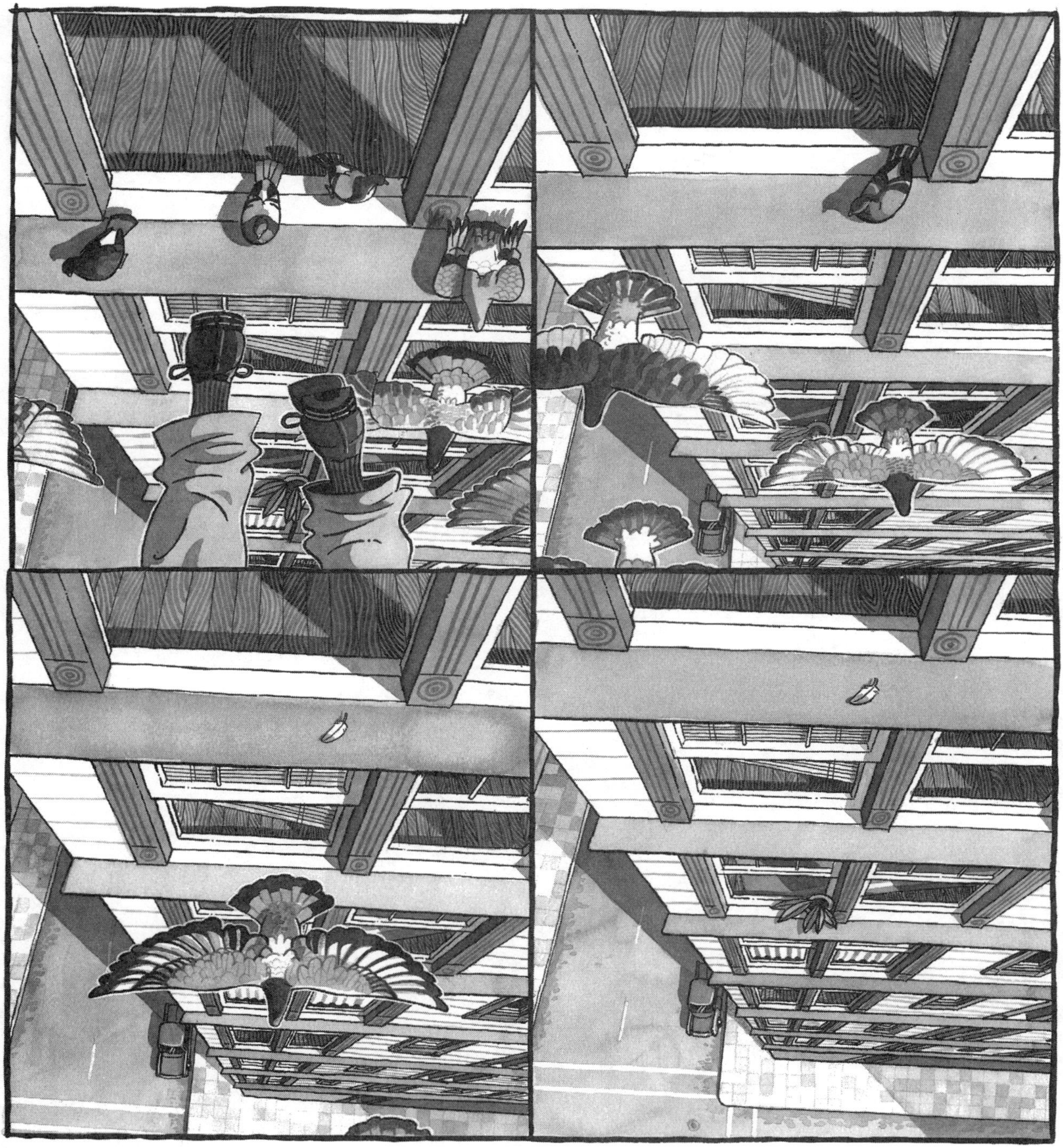

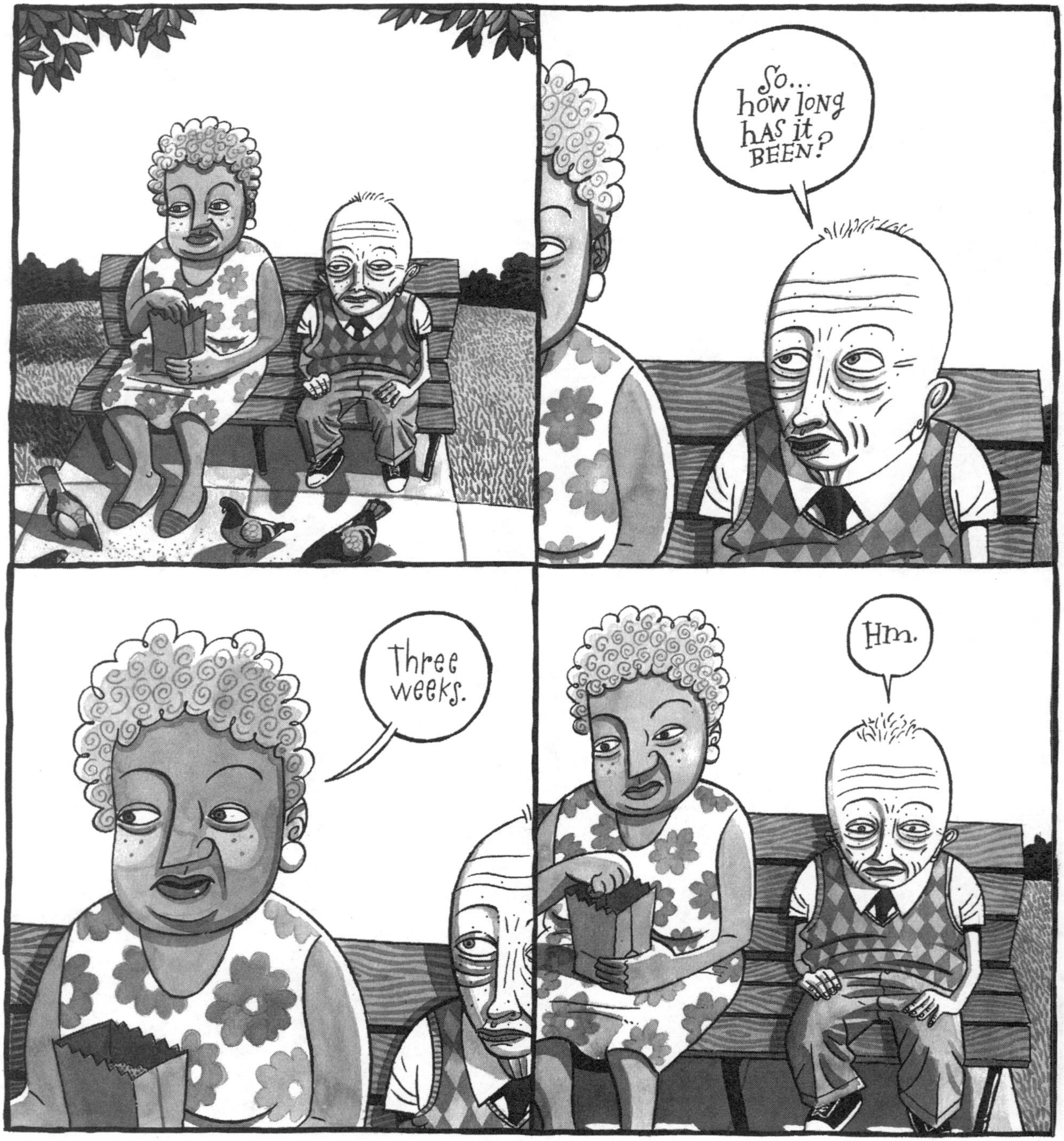
So... how long has it BEEN?
Three weeks.
Hm.

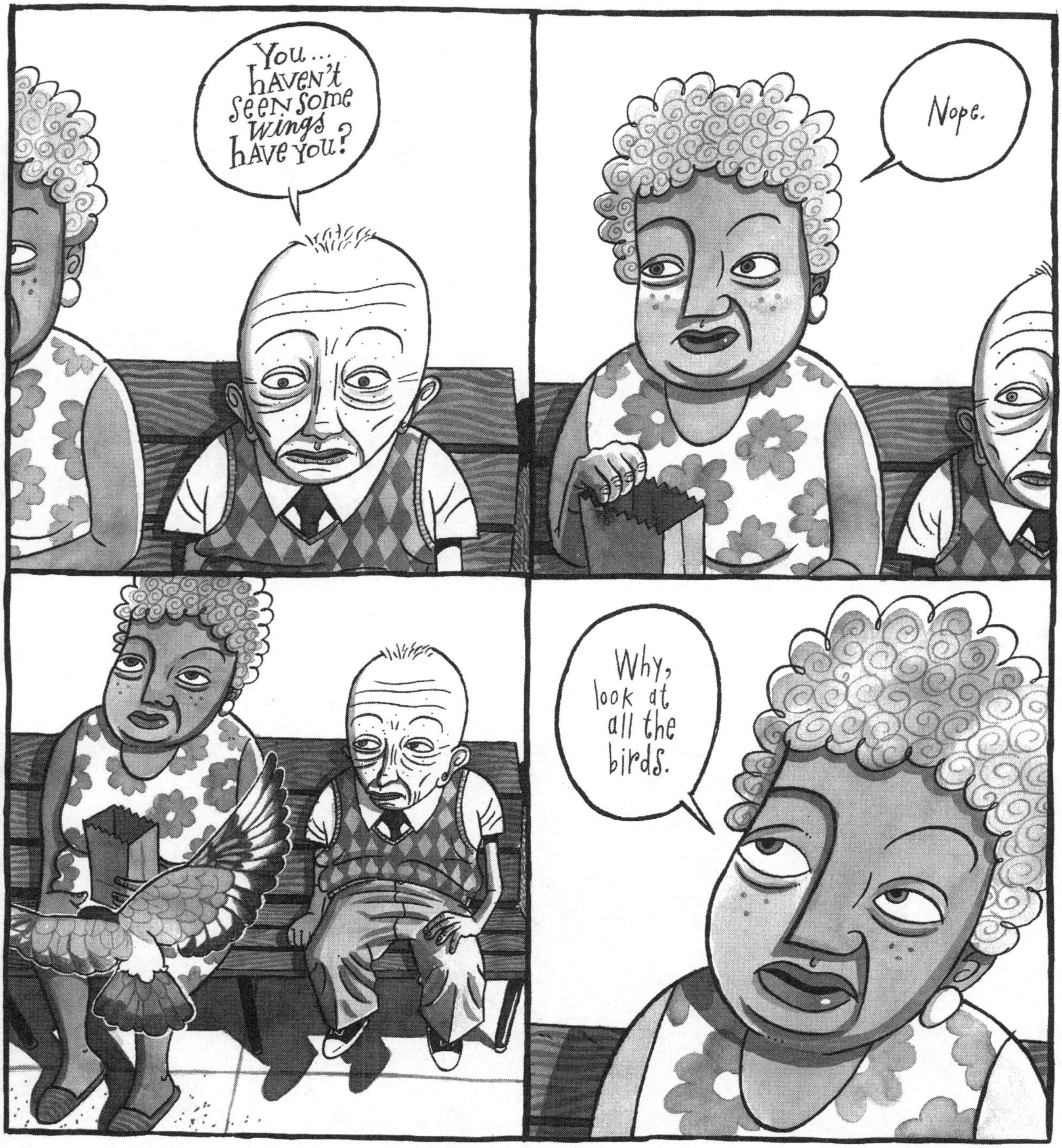
You... haven't seen some wings have you?
Nope.
Why, look at all the birds.

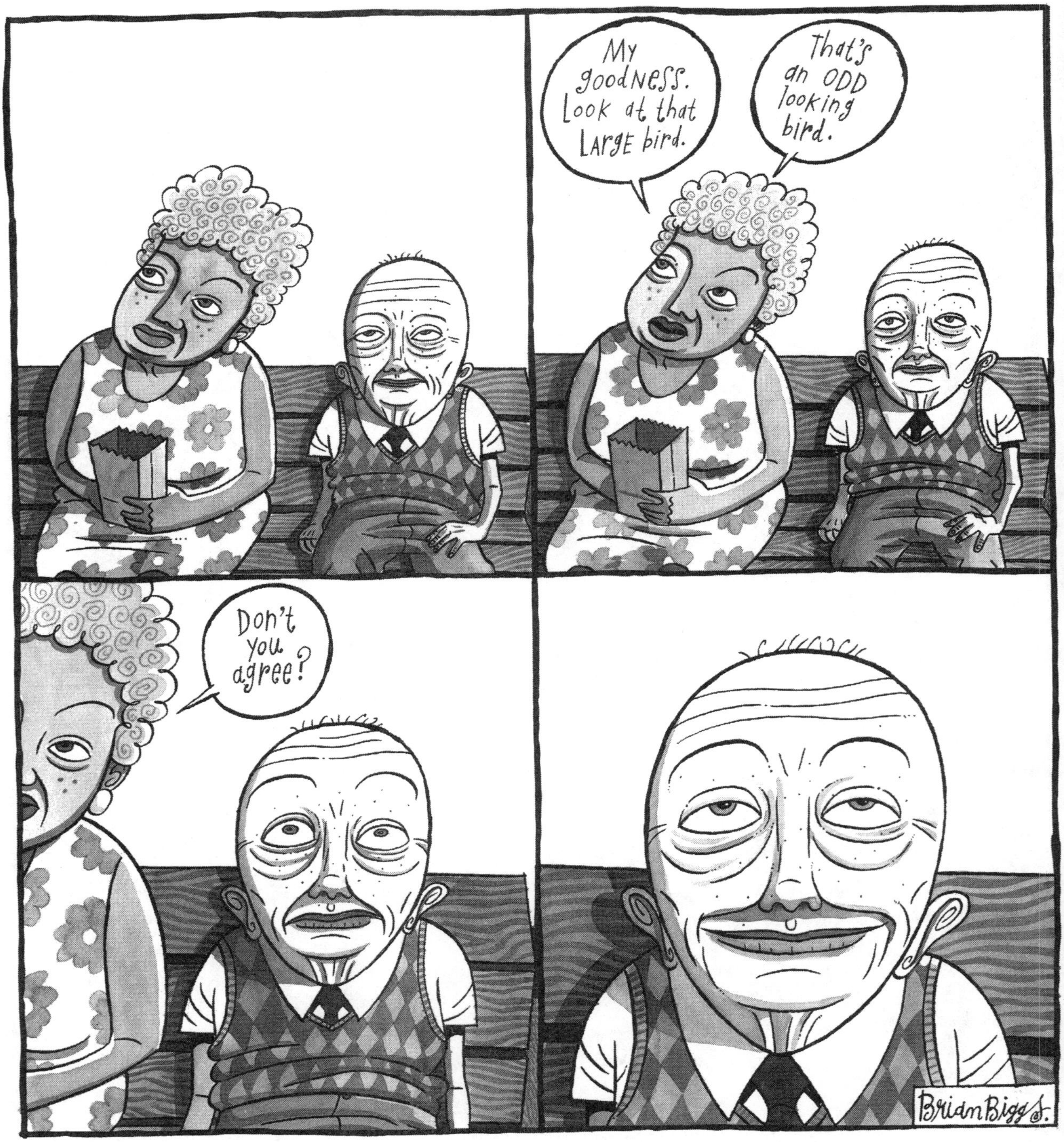
My goodNESS. Look at that LARGE bird.
That's an ODD looking bird.
Don't you agree?
BrianBiggs.

THE END

ABOUT THE AUTHOr:
Brian Biggs was born in 1968 in Little
Rock, Arkansas. He grew up in Texas,
spent some time in New York City,
Paris and San Francisco, and recently
landed in Philadelphia with his wife,
Jessica and their son, Wilson.
His previous work includes the book
Frederick & Eloise, published by
Fantagraphics in 1993, and many
other short works published in
various anthologies and magazines.
photo by Jacqueline Blackman